PRAISE FOR 24

"From pissoirs to parrots – M
24 Hours Paris by Prospera Pu........ .. ..
guide to Paris, chock full of unusual ideas for touring hidden
areas and attractions in the City of Light. Bravo to Marsha for
coming up with a totally new and creative way to
see my favourite town."

Doni Belau, *Founder,* www.girlsguidetoparis.com

"This incredible guidebook offers an hour-by-hour roadmap for
exploring the hidden wonders of this remarkable city, making it
a must-have ... even for people who think they know Paris."

Linda Donahue, *Editor-in-chief,* ParisienSalon.com

"For eons it seems travel writers have been telling us where
to go and what to do, but paid little heed to the other crucial
'w' – namely 'when'. Marsha Moore however has seized on the
importance of timing in illuminating the forgotten corners of
this great city, and whether you find yourself roaming the streets
at dawn or dusk you've only got to turn the page for inspiration.
Moore's guide to Paris is a real encyclopaedia of the hip and the
quirky, full of insider facts and trivia, that will banish all thoughts
of ennui for much longer than the stated 24 hours."

Duncan Rhodes, *Editor,* Urbantravelblog.com

"In spite of the fact I've lived in Paris for 22 years, this book
is a real eye-opener and I'm keeping it next to my bed in
case I awaken at 3 am and want to go out. I've read so many
guidebooks but this one has different take on the City of Light.
It's fun in addition to being illuminating. Marsha, thank you for
making Paris even more exciting."

Karen Fawcett, *President, Paris New Media, LLC,* www.bonjourparis.com

ABOUT THE AUTHOR

Marsha Moore first travelled to Paris when she was eighteen. She tried her best to fit in by wearing killer high heels, but her constant cobblestone-tripping somehow marked her out as a non-native.

Nevertheless, she remained determined to get to know Paris like a local – even if she'd never really possess that *je ne sais quoi*. **24 Hours Paris** is a result of her explorations into the Paris beyond the Eiffel Tower.

A native Canadian, Marsha has lived and worked in London, England, for the past six years. This is her second book in the *24 Hours series* after **24 Hours London** in 2009.

She is currently hard at work on a fiction title to be released next year.

MARSHA MOORE

2010/2011 Edition

PROSPERA
PUBLISHING

**Whilst every effort has been made to ensure the accuracy of
the listings contained in 24 Hours Paris, please note that the information
provided should be checked before visiting as venues, hours and
prices are subject to change constantly.**

ISBN 978-1-907504-01-3

A CIP catalogue record for this title is available from the British Library

Set in Segoe UI 11pt/13pt.

Printed and bound in the UK by Imprint.

Prospera Publishing.
Longreach, 36 Ashlyns Road, Berkhamsted HP4 3BL
editor@prosperapublishing.co.uk

INTRODUCTION

In a city like Paris, it's tempting to stick to the beautiful but beaten paths leading straight to the Eiffel Tower, Notre Dame and the Champs Elysée. But Paris is so much more than a collection of clichés; it's bursting with life, from early morning markets to midnight movies.

But how can you know where – and when – to get the best of what's beneath the city's gilded surface? The only thing for it is to break down the day, hour by hour, and make your choice from Paris' top picks.

That's exactly what **24 Hours Paris** does. Whether you're a foodie, a shopaholic, or in search of the city's quirkiest club, you'll see the best of what's on offer city-wide at any moment in time.

If you're up early, check out the morning hours for everything from one of the world's biggest food markets to urban jungles. Get a sugar rush from macarons, steer a train through city sights, and pucker up to kiss a literary legend. Want to shop? Browse unique creations in a covered arcade, buy the best kitchen gear where the chefs shop, or cut out the middleman and go direct at an artists' market.

Slow down the pace in the afternoon with a bit of culture, taking in Paris' amazing array of galleries and museums. If you need a break, get away from it all for a breather with Buddha, check out an underground garden or hang out in a fridge. Want to see purchase power in action? Head to an auction, where you can practice your French and buy antiques at the same time. Get a steam clean at France's largest mosque, or just relax with a cheeky pre-dinner drink with the art community. Rise above it all in a hot-air balloon, weave a tapestry or be a sewer rat: whatever you desire, you'll find it in **24 Hours Paris**.

Night-time's when Paris really comes into its own, with secret eats, floating films and ghost hunts. Take an anti-drawing lesson, munch a meal with opera, then jive to jazz in an underground torture chamber. Still feeling active? Roll around the city on rollerblades, swim under stars, then have a (baby) bottle with fondue to help you sleep.

To make your planning easier, each time-dependent activity is marked with an hour-glass. Opening hours, websites and contact information are always indicated where possible; for some of Paris' funkier venues, it's always best to call ahead to double check. Just flip to the hour you want, find the activity that catches your fancy, and turn on to the City of Light!

Marsha Moore, *London 2010*

CONTENTS

KEY

⧖ Varied or seasonal opening hours

🍽 Restaurant or food outlet

👨‍👧 Especially suitable for families

05:00

À la Mondrian

For a true tequila sunrise, head to **Le Mondrian**. Serving cocktails around the clock, it's a cosy place to duck into if you're craving something less polished than the usual Saint Germain fare. If you don't want to greet the sun with a hangover, grab one of their famous milkshakes and start off with some carbs instead.

Le Mondrian: 148 Boulevard Saint-Germain, 75006, +33 1 46 33 98 35. Métro: Mabillon or Odéon. Open: daily 9 am to 7 am.

Paris Projects

Begin the day with charitable thoughts at **45 Rue Jeanne d'Arc**. It's not much to look at, but this building is one of the earliest examples of social housing in Paris. Constructed by the *Société Philanthropique*, a society founded in 1780 by wealthy men 'inspired by benevolence', the building has housed people in difficulty since the mid-1800s – and it still does so today. The society now owns more than fifteen other buildings all over Paris, home to around 680 families.

The First Paris Project: 45 Rue Jeanne d'Arc, 75013. Métro: Nationale. www.philanthropique.asso.fr

Market with the Most

Billed as the largest fresh-produce wholesaler in the world, **Rungis Market** started life in the twelfth century at Les Halles. Known as the stomach of Paris, the legendary market fell into disrepair and in 1969 was relocated to the southern suburb of Rungis. Sadly, with its move went much of its convivial spirit. The new market is worth a look, though, even if just to marvel at its sheer size. Covering over 570 acres, with more than thirteen thousand people working there every day and selling almost two tonnes of goods annually, it's definitely the market with the most. Where else can you buy all your food groups before 7 am and some fresh flowers to boot?

Rungis Market: Rungis, 94152, +33 1 41 80 80 00. Métro: from Place d'Italie, take Métro line 7 to end of the line, then bus 185 to Rungis Market. Open: Mon to Sat, but check the website for specific market hours for fruits and vegetables, fish and seafood, meat, poultry and wild flowers, pots and decoration. www.rungisinternational.com

Squeeze In

Tighten your belt a notch and suck in your belly as you enter the narrowest street in Paris. At only 1.8 metres wide, to get through **Rue du Chat-qui-Pêche** – or the street of the fishing cat in English – you've got to cosy up to passers-by, whether you want to or not. There's not much to see in this narrow alleyway but if you're up for a challenge after breakfast, squeeze in!

Rue du Chat-qui-Pêche: between 9 Quai Saint-Michel and Rue de la Huchette, 75005. Métro: Saint-Michel. 👫

The Woman who Launched a Thousand Grains

Take to the water at **Pont de la Tournelle** and begin the day with a blessing from Saint Geneviève, the patron saint of Paris. Since 1928, her statue has sat atop a pylon on the eastern side of the bridge, keeping a watchful eye on her city. In 464, when the city was starving thanks to a blockade by a Merovingian king, Geneviève somehow managed to pass through the lines of boats and bring grain to the city. Showing their true appreciation of food, Parisians made her their patron saint.

Statue of Saint Geneviève: Quai de la Tournelle, 75006. Métro: Jussieu.

24 Hour Fact
Once around the inner loop on Noctilien night-bus Line 1 takes approximately one hour.

06:00

Take Charge

Grab hold of your destiny (or feel like it, anyway) on **Métro Line 14**. Get a seat right up front on these automated trains and pretend you're the one steering it down the track. Paris' Métro system is over a hundred years old, but Line 14 – opened in 1998 – is one of its newer offshoots. Take in the old-world glamour of the Gare de Lyon and Gare St Lazare, the Neoclassical elegance of the Church of the Madeleine and see the National Library of France, all from the comfort of the driver's seat.

Métro Line 14: check schedule at www.ratp.info. Trains generally run daily from 5:30 am to 1 am. 🚶‍♀️

Stay On Guard

Check out some artwork and monitor the Seine's water level at the same time. Resting on an old pile that used to support the Pont de l'Alma, the sculpture of a Zouave soldier is now the unofficial Parisian guide to floods. When the waters of the Seine reach his feet, the walkways lining the river banks are closed. If Zouave's thighs are wet, the Seine can't be navigated. During the Great Flood of 1910, water even reached Zouave's shoulders. Make like a Parisian and see if the city is in danger.

Zouave Statue: Pont de l'Alma, 75007. Métro: Alma-Marceau or Pont de l'Alma. 👫

Timber!

Contenders for the oldest houses in Paris, these half-timbered medieval buildings on **Rue François Miron** date from the fourteenth century. Narrow with steep roofs to drain rainwater, the timbers were only discovered during the 1960s when renovation workers peeled back the plaster to see wooden beams underneath (in 1607, Henri IV ordered all wood covered due to risk of fire). Get a glimpse of what Paris used to look like with these twin structures.

Oldest Houses in Paris: 11-13 Rue François Miron, 75004. Métro: Pont Marie or Saint Paul.

Walk On

To stroll on your own no matter the time, download an audio guide from **iAudioguide.com**. With 16 areas and attractions to explore, you can pound the pavement day or night. If you're venturing out in the dark, it's always a good idea to bring someone with you.

iAudioguide.com: www.iaudioguide.com. Price: 16 tracks for €4.95.

Old Bordello

It's just a generic building on a nothing-special street, but number **122 Rue de Provence** was once a prime destination for royalty, film stars and politicians – or anyone looking for a little bit of loving. In the 1930s, this townhouse was one of Paris' grandest bordellos and its rooms were designed to fulfil any man's dream, from getting it on in Rome to being nailed to a cross. The place to be seen at night, its restaurant also attracted icons like Marlene Dietrich, Charlie Chaplin and Katharine Hepburn. Solicitors toil away behind the windows now, but for those with vivid imaginations you can picture what once went on behind the closed doors and shutters.

Old Bordello: 122 Rue de Provence, 75008. Métro: Havre-Caumartin.

24 Hour Fact
With speeds up to 80 km per hour, Line 14 is Paris' fastest Métro line.

07:00

Get Sporty

To get your blood moving the good old-fashioned way, head to the tennis courts at the **Centre Sportif Suzanne Lenglen**. With fourteen courts (including two covered clay courts) plus a training wall, you can hit a ball around whatever the weather. And if tennis doesn't suit, this large sporting complex also has room for everything from rugby to basketball.

Centre Sportif Suzanne Lenglen: 2 Rue Louis Armand, 75015, +33 1 44 26 26 50. Métro: Balard. Open: Mon to Fri 7 am to 10 pm; Sat, Sun 7 am to 7 pm. Price: from €3. 🏃

Creation Location

Known as 'The Laundry Boat' because its poorly constructed walls and foundation swayed like a laundry boat on the Seine, the **Bateau-Lavoir** was one of the most famous artist squats in the world. Its low rent (there was no gas or electricity) attracted poor artists like Picasso, who took up residence there from 1904 to 1909. Other artists – including Amedeo Modigliani – followed, and the place became a central meeting point for everyone from Matisse to Braque, with the predictable flare of energy and inspiration. The tenement is reputedly the birthplace of the artistic movement known as Cubism, the style of painting for which Picasso is best known. A fire gutted the place in 1970 but it was rebuilt and is still used as an artist studio today. You won't be able to go inside, but there's a display in the front window outlining the building's eclectic history.

Bateau-Lavoir: 13 Rue Ravignan (Place Émile-Goudeau), 75018. Métro: Abbesses.

Go Courting

Just off busy St André des Arts, you can duck into a series of secret leafy courtyards many life-long Parisians still haven't discovered. Laced with ivy and dating back to before the sixteenth century, **La Cour de Rohan** was once home to Henry II's mistress, Diane de Poitiers, and more recently the painter Balthus. Keep your eyes peeled for the last *pas-de-mule* in Paris – a black wrought-iron structure in the middle courtyard, used to help overweight or elderly women get on their mules.

La Cour de Rohan: entrance off Boulevard Saint-Germain or Rue St André des Arts, 75006. Métro: Odéon.

Sugar-rush Hour

It's never too early to tickle your taste buds, and what better way to wake up to the world than with sugary sweet macarons? In Paris, you're rarely more than a stone's throw away from these vividly coloured drops of heaven, but if you're around Saint Germain it's worth popping into **Gérard Mulot**. Pick out your goodies, grab your little pink box and get ready for the sugar rush!

Gérard Mulot: 76 Rue de Seine, 75006, +33 1 43 26 85 77. Métro: Odéon. Open daily (except Wed) 6:45 am to 8 pm. www.gerard-mulot.com 🐡 👫

Float Away

Take a dip in a floating pool and wash away your worries at **La Piscine Joséphine Baker**. Named after the famous American performer and war heroine, the pool is the closest thing to swimming in the Seine itself – something that, with the current levels of pollution, is certainly not advisable. The pool draws its water from the river but don't be afraid: it undergoes a rigorous cleansing treatment first. With a retractable roof and sundeck, it's the ideal place for a summer-time splash but it's open all year too.

La Piscine Joséphine Baker: Quai François Mauriac, 75013, +33 1 56 61 96 50. Métro: Quai de la Gare, Bercy, Bibliothèque François Mitterrand. Open: Mon 7 am to 8:30 am, 1 pm to 9 pm; Tues 1 pm to 11 pm; Wed 7 am to 8:30 am, 1 pm to 9 pm; Thurs 1 pm to 11 pm; Fri 7 am to 8:30 am, 1 pm to 9 pm; Sat 11 am to 8 pm; Sun 10 am to 8 pm. Hours vary, especially during the summer and holidays; check website for details. Price: €3. http://piscines.paris.fr ⌛ 👫

Country Cat

Wake up to the world with a wander in a part of Paris that could be straight from the rural idylls. Located to the east of Parc des Buttes Charmont, the **Rue de Mouzaïa** and the narrow alleys running off it are bursting with trees and flowers. Houses are small and quaint, each painted different colours and nestling against the hill. Here, necessity fostered creativity: these two-storey constructions were all the land – unstable due to past quarrying – could support. Watch out for the many cats who call this place home as you stroll one of the most beautiful and unique residential areas of the city.

Les Villas de la Mouzaïa: Rue de Mouzaïa, 75019. Métro: Pré Saint-Gervais.

Expiration Date

Start the day with a reminder that life is precious by visiting the place where past greats like Princess Diana and Josephine Baker took their last breath. Built by order of Louis XIV in 1656, **Hôpital Pitié Salpêtrière** was once the largest hospital in the world. Doctors such as Sigmund Freud and Jean-Martin Charcot (a founding figure of modern neurology) both worked there, and famous past patients include Prince Ranier of Monaco, Michael Schumacher and Jacques Chirac. Fill your lungs and appreciate life.

Hôpital Pitié Salpêtrière: 47-83 Boulevard de l'Hôpital, 75013, +33 1 42 16 00 00. Métro: Saint-Marcel or Chevaleret. www.aphp.fr

Get Bus-y

Watch the city come to life and take in the sights from a commuter's-eye view on **Bus 72.** The route runs alongside the Seine and passes by many major Parisian landmarks, including the Eiffel Tower and the Palais de Chaillot as well as Les Invalides and Place de la Concorde. Sneak a peek into the Louvre before getting off at Hôtel de Ville. Reward yourself with a coffee and croissant: it may still be early but you've just done a day's worth of sightseeing in one go!

Route 72: buses run from Hotel de Ville to Parc de Saint-Cloud from 7 am until around 12 am. Check www.ratp.info for route and timetable information. Price for single-trip ticket: €1.60. 🏃

Pisstake

Relieve your bladder and get up close and personal with a piece of Parisian history at the same time. Located on Boulevard Arago in front of La Santé Prison, the city's last remaining **vespasienne** – otherwise known as *pissoir* – is the sole survivor of the 1,200 public urinals that once dotted the streets.

Nowadays, Parisians prefer the modern pod-like sanisettes, where toilet activities are out of sight to passers-by. But if privacy's no issue or if nature's call is too strong to resist then drop your trousers and engage with the past.

Last Pissoir: Boulevard Arago (in front of La Santé Prison), 75014. Métro: Saint-Jacques.

08:00

Writing on the Wall

See some art in the open on Belleville streets Dénoyez, Ramponeau and de l'Ermitage, where artists have transformed the city's plain urban surfaces into fantastical murals. Known collectively as **La Kommune**, this group of creatives has also taken over an abandoned theatre on Rue de l'Ermitage, covering the interior with graffiti, and a garden on Rue Ramponeau, where what's growing is as artistic as what's showing. If you go there for a Sunday afternoon stroll, you might even see the graffiti artists at work as the walls morph into their next incarnation.

La Kommune: 23-25 Rue Ramponeau, 75020. Métro: Belleville. www.lakommune.org

Sand and Seine

Most Parisians flee the city for the coast in August, but with **Paris-Plages** you can have your moment in the sun and stay in the big city too. First opened in 2002, the beach was decried as frivolous fun but Parisians soon embraced the concept with open arms – and swimsuits. Stretching over three kilometres, complete with sun loungers, palm trees, cafés and a swimming pool, you'll soon forget you're in the heart of a major metropolis. If you tire of relaxation, stretch your muscles with tai chi and wall-climbing. If it's your mind you're looking to exercise, head to one of Paris-Plages' other locations at the **François Mitterrand National Library**, where you can read a newspaper for free, take out a book, use the Internet and even learn how to draw. Just keep your suit on, ladies – topless bathing is not *de rigueur*.

Paris-Plages: Pont Neuf to Pont de Sully, 75001. Métro: Pont Neuf. Also at François Mitterrand National Library, Quai Mauriac, 75013. Métro: Quai de la Gare, Bibliothèque François Mitterrand; and Bassin de la Villette, 75019. Métro: Jaurès. All open: from around the 20th July for four weeks, daily 8 am to 12 am. ⧗ �

Sweet Breads

The debate over Paris' best bakery rages on, but **Poilâne** is a definite contender. Opened in 1932 by the young Pierre Poilâne from Normandy, Poilâne's bread has stood the test of time. Baked in a wood-fired oven the same way they always have been, the traditional sourdough loaves were so popular Salvador Dalí once ordered a whole bedroom made out of them! Bite in to see if they live up to your bread expectations. And if you love the bread so much you can't live without it, never fear – you can take away a cushion shaped exactly like a Poilâne loaf and fill your head with sweet bread dreams.

Poilâne: 8 Rue du Cherche-Midi, 75006, +33 1 45 48 42 59. Métro: Vaneau, Saint-Placide. Open: Mon to Sat 7:15 am to 8:15 pm. www.poilane.fr 🚲�

Get Hopping

Things move fast at **Porte de Montreuil**, one of the oldest and largest flea markets in Paris, where you can find everything from car-parts to second-hand clothes. The mountains of tat may not be pretty, but sifting through the piles just might unearth a treasure: in 1991, a punter reputedly bought a painting here that later turned out to be a Van Gogh worth over two million Euro! Go early on a Monday morning before all the good stuff is snatched up.

Porte de Montreuil Market: Avenue de la Porte de Montreuil, 75020. Métro: Porte de Montreuil. Open: Sat to Mon 7 am to 6 pm.

Sacred Sandwich

If you need some fortification before making the climb to the Sacré Coeur Cathedral, head over to bakery **Coquelicot**. Grab one of their takeaway sandwiches to munch on while you toil – or, if you prefer not to mix pleasure with *pain*, simply collapse on the hilly lawns on the way up to the cathedral and enjoy. Coquelicot also offers a filling brunch but be warned: you may not feel like moving afterwards! Grab a baguette to dip in your hot chocolate, relax in the flower-dotted interior, and enjoy.

Coquelicot: 24 Rue des Abbesses, 75018, +33 1 46 06 18 77. Métro: Abbesses. Open: daily 7:30 am to 8 pm. Brunch served 8 am to 6 pm (winter); to 7 pm (summer). www.coquelicot-montmartre.com

Hit It!

Practise your swing and improve your game at the **Golf du Bois de Boulogne**. With a driving range of almost 250 metres, a 'crazy golf' course complete with bunkers and water obstacles as well as a putting green, there's no excuse for going over par. Prices start at €4 for 28 balls and you can even take a half-hour lesson for €25.

Golf du Bois de Boulogne: Hippodrome d'Auteuil, 75016, +33 1 44 30 70 00. Métro: Porte d'Auteuil. Open: mid-Sept to Apr daily 8 am to 8 pm; May to mid-Sept daily 8 am to 9 pm. Closed on course days; check website for details. Price: €4. www.golfduboisdeboulogne.fr ⌛ ♁

Sceaux What?

You may think it's just another park in the hinterland beyond the Paris periphery, but **Parc de Sceaux** entices even the most hardcore Parisians out of the city. The park's château is surrounded by immaculate grounds (designed by André Le Nôtre, famed for his work at Versailles), making it a perfect place to stretch out and take in the view.

After your siesta, you can stroll by the Grand Canal, relax by the fountains or grab a crêpe from one of the food-stands.

Feeling adventurous? Take your chances and try to catch a fish in the canal. If you tire of country life, the town of Sceaux is worth a visit in itself, with bakeries, shops and bookstores.

Parc de Sceaux: Sceaux, 92330, +33 1 41 87 28 00. Métro: RER Line B, station Bourg-la-Reine, Parc de Sceaux, Croix-de-Berny or Sceaux. Open: daily from 7 am (summer) or 8 am (winter) but times change from month to month, check the website for details. Fishing permitted with valid licence, not permitted from 2 pm on Sat, Sun. http://parc.de.sceaux.free.fr 🍷🎣👫

Fountain Fantastic

You may think you're still dreaming when you see the surreal structures of the **Stravinsky Fountain**, but rub the sleep from your eyes and watch as the 16 colourful pieces – inspired by Igor Stravinsky's music – spout water and move. Built in 1983 by Jean Tinguely and Niki de Saint Phalle, the mechanical sculptures include a firebird, a frog, death and the musical key of G. Ease yourself into reality with these whimsical creations.

Stravinsky Fountain: Place Igor Stravinsky (next to Centre Pompidou), 75004. Métro: Rambuteau. 👫

Piece of Britain

If you need a bit of Blighty, head over to **Place Edouard VII** where you can find a piece of England without leaving Paris. The son of Queen Victoria, Edward VII made a nearby hotel (now fittingly named Hotel Edouard VII) his home-base in Paris, and a theatre in the area also bears his name.

As he waited to ascend to the throne after his mother Queen Victoria, Edward became an expert in the art of leisure and quickly found Paris to be the ideal place to satisfy his desires.

Fully fluent in French – and possessing great charm and a fashion sense to match – Edward was responsible for making tweed fashionable amongst Parisians, as well as making it *en vogue* to wear black ties with dinner jackets.

A patron of the arts (and an ardent pursuer of actresses and singers) up until his death in 1910, French authorities erected a statue of Edward on a horse here in his honour. Pay homage to a royal whose Francophilia had a lasting impression.

Place Edouard VII: 82 Rue Edouard VII, 75009. Métro: Opéra.

Lotta Love

Set your sights on love at the **I Love You Wall.** The brainchild of Frédéric Baron, the wall consists of over 1000 'I love yous' written in more than 300 languages. Assembled by artists Claire Kito and Daniel Boulogne on 612 tiles of enameled lava, the wall is not just about love: the splashes of colour here and there represent broken hearts. Grab a coffee and start the day with a little – or a lot of, in this case – love.

Le Mur des Je t'aime: Square Jehan-Rictus, Place des Abbesses, 75018. Métro: Abbesses. Open: daily, 24 hours. Price: free. www.lesjetaime.com

09:00

Oui Chef!

Learn to recreate a taste of Paris at home with **Eye Prefer Paris'** cooking classes. Expert Paris blogger Richard Nahem will help you choose the best ingredients at a local market. Then, you'll cook up a storm under the watchful eye of professional chef Charlotte Puckette, author of *The Ethnic Paris Cookbook*. Better still, once you're done you can feast on your creation with the perfect wine. After all that, what you've learned might be a wee bit fuzzy but your taste buds will be eternally grateful. Locations depend on the class chosen.

Cooking Classes: Eye Prefer Paris. Classes held Wed to Sun from 9:30 am to 2 pm. Price: €185 per person; minimum 3 people, maximum 6. www.eyepreferparistours.com/cooking-class ⏳🍴

Mini-Me Liberty

You might not expect to find such a famous American icon residing in Paris, but the city is home to two miniature Statues of Liberty. French sculptor Frédéric Auguste Bartholdi designed the great lady, apparently casting the face of his mother with the body of his lover. Head to the

Luxembourg Gardens to check out Bartholdi's first model of Lady Liberty, or to the Pont de Grenelle where the bronze statue rises twenty-two metres above the Allées des Cygnes. First unveiled in 1889, Bartholdi complained she was facing east, away from America. The Lady was finally turned in 1937 to face the States but Bartholdi never lived to see it.

When you're done gazing at the statue, take a stroll down Allées des Cygnes on the artificial **Île des Cygnes** (Island of Swans), originally constructed as a dam to protect the port of Grenelle. Head towards Bir-Hakeim Bridge, arguably one of the most photogenic – and famous – bridges in Paris, having made appearances in *Last Tango in Paris* as well as Janet Jackson's video *Come Back to Me*.

Luxembourg Gardens: access from Boulevard Saint-Michel, Rue de Vaugirard, Rue Guynemer, Rue Auguste Comte, Rue de Médicis. Métro: Notre-Dames-des-Champs. Open: hours vary by season; check website for details. www.paris.fr ⧗

Pont de Grenelle: 75015, 75016. Métro: Passy or Bir-Hakeim.

Go Green

Want something different to ease your headache? Go to **Pharmacie Zagorski**, where head pharmacist Annie has been mixing up plant-based remedies for over thirty years. With a plethora of plant products made in-house, along with a variety of traditional pharmaceuticals, you can find everything from wheat-germ oil to ibuprofen. When the norm doesn't work, why not go *au naturel*?

Pharmacie Zagorski: 6 Rue Jacob, 75006, +33 1 43 26 99 69. Métro: Saint-Germain-des-Prés or Mabillon. Open: Mon to Sat 9 am to 7:30 pm. www.pharmaciezagorski.com

Sax it Up

It's one of the world's best-loved instruments, so take a second to pay homage to Adolphe Sax, creator of – you guessed it – the saxophone. Born in 1814 in Belgium, Sax moved to Paris in 1841. He began work on a new kind of instrument: the precursor to the modern-day saxophone. In 1846 the saxophone was patented and Sax made his name in the world of music, teaching students to play his new instrument at the Paris Conservatoire. He died in 1894 after going bankrupt twice to defend his patent. You can visit this musical inventor in section five of the **Montmartre Cemetery**, where he rests in good company with ballet legend Vaslav Nijinsky, novelist Alexandre Dumas (son) and film-maker François Truffaut.

Grave of Adolphe Sax: section 5, Cimetière Montmartre, 20 Avenue Rachel, 75018, +33 1 53 42 36 30. Métro: Place de Clichy or Blanche. Open: Mon to Fri 8 am to 6 pm; Sat 8:30 am to 6 pm; Sun 9 am to 6 pm (until 5:30 pm in winter). Price: free.

Market Mania

With over three thousand stalls at the **Saint-Ouen Flea Market**, you might lose more than a few Euros – you might lose your mind. Opened in 1885, the flea market is composed of several smaller markets specialising in everything from vintage surgical instruments to the latest street wear. It's in antiques, though, that Saint-Ouen really shines. Head to the Biron section for the market's 'Faubourg St-Honoré' (read: expensive) section, with tapestries and furniture from the eighteenth to the twentieth centuries. If Art Deco's more your speed, scoot over to the Rosiers market. Or if you've always coveted a Napoleon-style hat, go to Jules Valles, the oldest covered market in Saint-Ouen. Chances are if you can't find whatever it is you're looking for here, it doesn't exist.

Les Puces de Paris Saint-Ouen: Avenue de la Porte de Clignancourt, 93400, Saint-Ouen, +33 1 40 12 32 58. Métro: Porte de Clignancourt. Open: Saturdays, Sundays and Mondays, including Bank Holidays, from 9:30 am to 6 pm. Thursday and Friday mornings are reserved for trade professionals. www.parispuces.com ⌛ 👫

Plant Power

Rise above it all and surround yourself with an oasis of calm on the **Promenade Plantée**. This once-abandoned railway track is now a 4.5 kilometre-long elevated walking route from Bastille to the Bois de Vincennes. Created in 1988, you can expect to get up close and personal with the urban and the wild as you pass by buildings and bats (the *Pipistrelle* hangs out here). Walk amidst the wild poppies, cherry trees and wrought-iron balconies, take in the great views over the roof-tops, and savour the urban jungle.

Promenade Plantée: take the steps up from 290 Avenue Daumesnil (south of Bastille Opera House), 75012. Métro: Bastille. Open: Mon to Fri from 8 am; Sat, Sun from 9 am to 5:30 pm (Jan); 6 pm (Feb); 7 pm (Mar); 9 pm (Apr, May); 9:30 pm (June, July); 8:30 pm (Sept). Price: free. ⌛ 👫

Go Cerf-ing

Built in 1825, the covered arcade of **Passage du Grand Cerf** is one hundred metres of pure shopping glee. With thirty-three shops ranging from the latest designers to artists' workshops, you'll be sure to find something unlike any other. Check out MX Sylvie Branellec, whose pearl-crafted jewellery shines under a giant crab ceiling. Or head to Le Labo for lights like you've never seen, fashioned from fabric and wire or reclaimed objects. Whatever the shop, your senses will be satisfied – even though it'll likely be at the expense of your pocketbook!

Passage du Grand Cerf: 145 Rue Saint-Denis and 8 Rue Dussoubs, 75002. Métro: Étienne Marcel. Open: Mon to Sat 8:30 am to 8 pm. www.passagedugrandcerf.com

Stop and Croque

An old-school café with a large terrace overlooking Saint-Sulpice church, **Café de la Mairie** is a great place to stop for some caffeine and a Croque Monsieur (made with the legendary Poilâne bread). The café is said to have been Henry Miller's favourite and it's still popular with well-known figures today: Catherine Deneuve reputedly takes her coffee here, too.

Café de la Mairie: 8 Place Saint-Sulpice, 75006, +33 1 43 26 67 82. Métro: Saint-Sulpice. Open: Mon to Fri 7 am to 2 am; Sat 8 am to 2 am; Sun 9 am to 9 pm.

Step it Up

Kick into high gear at dance school **Studio Harmonic** where you can learn to do the moonwalk and other assorted Jackson moves; dance the Ragga Jam (a mix of African and Jamaican steps); or embrace tradition with some classical ballet. If you want to stay grounded, stretch your muscles with yoga. Whatever your style, if you're looking to move then this is your place.

Studio Harmonic: 5 Passage des Taillandiers, 75011, +33 1 48 07 13 39. Métro: Bastille. Office open: Mon to Fri 10 am to 5 pm. Classes Mon to Fri 9:30 am to 10 pm; Sat 9 am to 7:30 pm. www.studioharmonic.fr

Back to Basics

If you're after the freshest produce grown organically, fill your basket at the **Marché Biologique Batignolles**. Specialising in all things organic, you can pick up anything from peas to raw silk and throw in a little fish for fun. This weekly market overflows with vivid colours and items to satisfy both eyes and stomach.

Marché Biologique Batignolles: middle of Boulevard de Batignolles, 75008. Métro: Rome or Place de Clichy. Open: Sat 9 am to 2 pm. ⧗

Dishpan Hands

You won't be able to keep your mitts off the kitchenware at **E. Dehillerin**. Supplying chefs and cooking enthusiasts since 1820, the store has everything you need to keep you happy in the kitchen for hours – whether you're cooking or not! From copper pots to duck presses, you'll find things you didn't even know existed. Don't be fooled by the store's down-to-earth appearance, though: it is not reflected in the (very) high prices!

E. Dehillerin: 18-20 Rue Coquillière, 75001, +33 1 42 36 53 13. Métro: Les Halles. Open: Mon 9 am to 12:30 pm and 2 pm to 6 pm; Tues to Sat 9 am to 6 pm. www.e-dehillerin.fr ⏳

Go Wilde

Get your lipstick on and pucker up to kiss the tomb of Oscar Wilde at **Père Lachaise Cemetery**. The notorious Irish playwright died in Paris in 1900, having left Britain a few years earlier after his release from jail for gross indecency. The original rebel, Wilde had numerous relationships with both men and women, refusing to conform to Victorian standards. Leave your mark of admiration for one of the most famous men of his time.

To get even more amorous, go to the tomb of Victor Noir. A journalist killed by Pierre Napoleon Bonaparte, the penis on his life-like stone form seems to be in a permanent state of arousal. The tomb has become a fertility symbol, with women rubbing his nether-regions in hopes of getting pregnant.

Put a flower in his hat, kiss his lips then slip a hand down under and your hopes might just come true.

Graves of Oscar Wilde and Victor Noir: Cimetière Père Lachaise, Boulevard de Ménilmontant, 75020. Métro: Gambetta (closest to the grave of Oscar Wilde), Père-Lachaise. Open: Mon to Fri 8 am to 6 pm; Sat 8:30 am to 6 pm; Sun 9 am to 6 pm (until 5:30 pm in winter). Price: free. www.pere-lachaise.com

Backseat Driver

Tour Paris in a piece of French history itself, the Citroën 2CV. Produced between 1948 to 1990, these *deux chevaux vapeur* (two steam horses, in English) are considered by many to be an icon of French cars – James Bond himself even drove one in the 1981 film *For Your Eyes Only*. With **Paris Authentic's 2CV Tours**, you can be the star of your own show.

Choose from a variety of tours by day or by night and take in the sights through the open-top or see-through roof. Snuggle up in the back seat and let the knowledgeable guide (and the two steam horses) do all the work.

2CV Paris Tour: +33 664 504 419, infos@parisauthentic.com. Pick up and drop off from hotel or address in Paris centre. Tours arranged to suit your schedule. Prices start from €40 per person for a two-hour tour for three people. www.parisauthentic.com ⌛

10:00

Forgive Not Forget

Two hundred thousand French were deported to Nazi concentration camps during the Second World War. Opened in 1962, the **Mémorial des Martyrs de la Déportation** commemorates those who lost their lives. Built on the site of a former morgue, its long underground tunnels and dark, cramped chambers are designed to induce a claustrophobic feeling. In the gloom, the 200,000 light crystals that line the walls seem that much brighter and the glow of the eternal flame more poignant. The inscription 'Forgive, but never forget' at the exit implores visitors to never again let history repeat itself.

Mémorial des Martyrs de la Déportation: Square de l'Ile de France, 75004, +33 1 46 33 87 56. Métro: Cité. Open: winter daily 10 am to 12 pm, 2 pm to 5 pm; summer daily 10 am to 12 pm, 2 pm to 7 pm. Price: free.

Seduction Instruction

Frenchmen are famous for their romantic nature but it doesn't come naturally to everyone. If you want to learn the fine art of seduction, sign up for master seducer Sébastien Night's **Seduction Classes**. One-on-one or in group seminars, you can learn to overcome your shyness and approach women in any situation. Once you've mastered that, enrol in the 'Dolce Vita' course and practise your superior skills by cruising through six European cities. Life is sweet, indeed.

Séduction by Night: +33 6 67 31 49 44 (lines open from 9 am to 12 pm), seminaires@topgun-seduction.com. Check website for details of upcoming courses; usually held at 10 am. www.seduction-bynight.com ⧗

Hit the Books

Browse some old titles on the site of a former vineyard turned slaughterhouse turned park. Although it has a bloody history, **Parc Georges Brassens** is now a peaceful space complete with a large rose garden and a Garden of Scents, featuring more than 80 kinds of aromatic spices and plants. The real attraction, though, is the weekend market when over 60 booksellers flog their literary wares in the old horse stalls. Take a page from the past and sit amongst the flowers in a park with as much of a story as the book you're holding.

Market Georges Brassens: Parc Georges Brassens, 104 Rue Brancion, 75015. Métro: Convention or Porte de Vanves. Market held every Sat and Sun from 9 am to 6 pm. www.gippe.org/marche_du_livre ⧗

Go Big and Go Rex

If you fancy a film to start the day, you can't go wrong at **Le Grand Rex**. Although the films are in French, it's worth a visit to see this cinema's decadent wedding cake exterior. The inside is nothing to sneer at either – with over 2,700 seats, it's supposedly the largest cinema in Europe, with the biggest screen, too. If you're around in April, pop by for the annual Jules Verne Adventure Film Festival when more than 48,000 attendees flood the cinema. Even if you're not a film fanatic, you can't help but be impressed.

Le Grand Rex: 1 Boulevard Poissonnière, 75002, +33 1 08 92 68 05 96. Métro: Bonne Nouvelle. Morning films usually start around 10:15 am; check website for details. www.legrandrex.com ⏳ 👫

Tasty Tang

You'd expect the biggest Chinese supermarket chain west of China to be chock-full of Asian delights, and **Tang Frères** does not disappoint. Located in the 13th arrondissement of Paris – home to Paris' Chinatown – Tang Frères' shelves are stocked with everything from smelly durians to colourfully wrapped sweets. Avoid weekends when the crowds of shoppers, maze-like aisles and mix of exotic smells threaten to overwhelm. This supermarket apparently has more daily visitors than the Pompidou Centre!

Tang Frères: 48 Avenue d'Ivry, 75013, +33 1 45 70 80 00. Métro: Porte d'Ivry. Open: Tues to Sun 9 am to 7:30 pm.

Crazy for Coffee

If the heady smell of roasting coffee beans doesn't get you, one look at the quaint, coffee-bean-stuffed interior will lure you inside. **Café Verlet** has been giving caffeine-starved Parisians their coffee fix since 1880 and it couldn't be more different from its chain-gang neighbours if it tried. Choose from a menu of coffees from the Yemen to Brazil, or splash out for a rare gourmet bean from Australia. No matter what you go for, you're sure to leave here with a buzz!

Café Verlet: 256 Rue Saint-Honoré, 75001, +33 1 42 60 67 39. Métro: Palais Royale-Musée du Louvre. Open: Mon to Sat 9 am to 7 pm. Closed August. www.cafesverlet.com 🦐

Mooch around Mouffetard

Dating back to Neolithic times when it was a thoroughfare winding its way to Italy, **Rue Mouffetard** is a little piece of *le vrai Paris*. Protected from Baron Haussmann's massive redevelopment efforts in the mid-nineteenth century due to its awkward location on the side of a hill, Rue Mouffetard's narrow cobbled track – framed by small specialty food shops – is a slice of the past. Grab a coffee in the picturesque Place de la Contrescarpe (immortalised in novels by Hemingway and Balzac), then browse your way down the street, stopping at the morning fruit and vegetable market at the bottom. The market is at its peak on Sundays between ten and twelve.

Rue Mouffetard: 75005. Métro: Place Monge or Censier-Daubenton. Most shops closed from Sunday at 12 pm until Tuesday at 10 am. Market on every morning but Monday from around 9 am to 12 pm.

Mane Master

From beards to barnets, **Alain Mâitre Barbier** is an expert in all things hair. His vintage-style shop – with artefacts from barbershops of the past – is worth a visit as much as his legendary barber skills.

Learn from the master with his one-on-one shaving lessons, or just sit back, get slathered with a badger brush, and emerge a new man!

Alain Mâitre Barbier: 8 Rue Saint-Claude, 75003, +33 1 42 77 55 80. Métro: Saint-Sébastien - Froissart. Open: Mon to Fri 9:15 am to 7 pm; Sat 9:15 am to 6 pm. By appointment only. www.maitrebarbier.com ⌛

Bastille Steal

The largest artists' market in Paris, **Bastille Artists' Market** has only been around since 2004 but it is now a firm Saturday fixture. With over 200 exhibitors selling everything from stained glass to sculptures, you can be sure what you buy here is truly an original.

Cut out the middleman and go direct as you get up close and personal with inspiration and creation.

Bastille Artists' Market: Boulevard Richard Lenoir, 75011. Métro: Bastille. Open: Sat 10 am to 7 pm. www.artistesparisbastille.fr ⌛

Glassy Eyed

The sheer amount of sparkling glass on display at the **Baccarat Museum** is almost blinding. Founded in 1764 in the French town of Baccarat, Baccarat Crystal has produced everything from candelabras to hookahs for a long line of royal houses around the world. Some of its finest treasures are now on display in the former mansion of a viscountess, redesigned in seriously over-the-top style by Philippe Starck.

Check out the crystal chandelier submerged in water, the talking vases and pieces specially designed for the Prince of Wales.

Galerie-musée Baccarat: 11 Place des Etats-Unis, 75116, +33 1 40 22 11 00. Métro: Iéna, Boissière. Open: Mon, Wed to Sat 10 am to 6:30 pm. Price: €5. www.baccarat.fr

Off With Their Heads!

Still used today to mete out justice as part of the Palais de Justice, **La Conciergerie** is best known as a prison whose most famous resident was Marie Antoinette. Built in the fourteenth century as a royal palace, it was converted to a prison in 1391 after the royal family took up fancier digs across the river.

When the French Revolution rolled around, La Conciergerie gained infamy as the last stop before the guillotine – around 2,600 prisoners were sent off to the chop from here.

Have a look at Marie Antoinette's former cell (now a chapel dedicated to her memory) and the kitchen with five fireplaces, each big enough to roast an entire ox.

La Conciergerie: 2 Boulevard du Palais, 75001, +33 1 53 40 60 80. Métro: Châtelet, Saint Michel, Cité. Open: Mar to Oct daily 9:30 am to 6 pm; Nov to Feb daily 9 am to 5 pm. Price: €7; €4.50 concession; under 18s free when accompanied by adult. http://conciergerie.monuments-nationaux.fr 🏃

Get Some Space

Forget earthly delights and revel in the skies at the **Musée de l'Air et de l'Espace** (Air and Space Museum). Climb aboard a Concorde, check out a Boeing 747 or land a plane from World War II – and if you're eager for more, browse the museum's collection of acrobatic planes. If you really fancy heaven, head to the planetarium where you can fill your eyes with stars.

Musée de l'Air et de l'Espace: Aéroport de Paris-Le Bourget, +33 1 49 92 70 62. Métro: Take 350 bus from Gare du Nord; or the 152 from Port de la Villette. Open: Apr to Sept, Tues to Sun, 10 am to 6 pm; Oct to Mar, Tues to Sun, 10 am to 5 pm. Price: €6, €4 under 26s. Planetarium open Wed 2 pm, 2:45 pm, 3:45 pm; Sat, Sun and school holidays 11 am, 11:45 am, 2 pm, 2:45 pm. Price: €5, €3 under 26s. www.mae.org 🏃

Pine for Poets

Take a walk alongside your favourite poets at the **Square des Poètes**. Mixing nature with literature, you can stroll amongst the flowers and forty-eight plaques bearing excerpts by legends like Baudelaire and Molière. The tallest Austrian pine in Paris (thirty two metres!) looks down on busts of Victor Hugo and Alexander Pushkin. There's also a playground and a sandbox to keep the young ones entertained as you ponder the poems.

Square des Poètes: Avenue du Général Sarrail, 75016. Métro: Porte d'Auteuil. www.paris.fr

Eye Candy

Can't focus? Need to fit in with the über-cool, sunglasses-sporting crowd? **Alain Mikli**'s frames will transform your vision, if not your life. Choose from the Swarovski-encrusted 'shutter shades' specially designed for music star Kanye West, or the 'candy' glasses with frames made from cellulose acetate in eye-popping colours. With clients like Elton John and Catherine Deneuve, it's the place to go to look like a star.

Alain Mikli: 74 Rue des Saints-Pères, 75007, +33 1 45 49 40 00. Métro: Sèvres-Babylone, Saint-Sulpice. Open: Mon to Sat 10 am to 7 pm. www.mikli.fr

In Gratitude

If you've ever hankered after the possibility of shopping guilt-free, head straight to **Merci**. Although nothing here's cheap, all profits on the designer-donated items go straight to charity. The creation of Marie-France Cohen, the woman behind Bonpoint, Merci's 1500-square-metres of shopping space in a converted factory is filled with perfume, home decorations and clothes, to name a few. Shop to your heart's content and remember: it's all for a good cause!

Merci: 111 Boulevard Beaumarchais, 75003, +33 1 42 77 00 33. Métro: Saint-Sébastien – Froissart. Open: Mon to Sat 10 am to 7 pm. www.merci-merci.com

Space Invaders

Fancy a peak into a private square? Access to Paris' infamous fashion houses, or a meeting with a master of art? You're in luck: with **Paris Privé**, you can do this – and more. The organisation arranges for individuals to visit otherwise inaccessible locations, from seeing the kitchen of a master chef to piloting a boat on the waterways. Lift the lid on the City of Light and experience first-hand what a life of luxury is all about.

Paris Privé: 34 Avenue des Champs Elysées, 75008, +33 1 42 56 27 59. Métro: Franklin D. Roosevelt. Prices and times vary depending on tour chosen. www.parisprive.com ⧗

French Justice

Watch a little French justice in action at the **Palais de Justice**, the home of Paris' Court of Appeal and Large-Claims Court, as well as France's Supreme Court. Pass through the security check (make sure not to have any sharp objects and have some ID), then choose a court-room to see if the law sounds any better in French.

With 24 kilometers of corridors and seven thousand doors, there's plenty to explore even if you're not a legal eagle.

Palais de Justice: 4 Boulevard du Palais, 75001, +33 1 44 32 52 52. Métro: Cité or Saint Michel. Open: Mon to Fri 9 am to 6 pm. www.ca-paris.justice.fr

Crazy House

Known by neighbours as Castle Dérangé (deranged), this infamous house designed by Hector Guimard in 1898 is considered to be one of the first examples of Art Nouveau architecture. With its bizarre mix of materials, **Castel Béranger** made Guimard's name and led to him winning a contract to design the entrances of some Métro stations, for which he is now famous. Check out the surreal water fountain in the courtyard, then head up the street to Hotel Mezzara at number 60, also designed by Guimard.

Although he died in exile and his works were largely forgotten until he was rediscovered in the 1960s, these houses stand as exuberant reminders of creativity and originality.

Castel Béranger: 14 Rue la Fontaine, 75016. Métro: Ranelagh or Jasmin. House not open to public.

24 Hours of Romance

11:00

Pet a Parrot

If you're tired of examining inanimate objects, go to the **Quai de la Mégisserie** for some live attractions. Selling everything from parrots to ferrets, the pet stores lining this stretch of the Seine will tug the strings of even the most hardened hearts. Formerly a foul-smelling area where sheep were skinned, the quay now reverberates with the sounds of exotic birds and the heady smell of blossoms from the multitudes of flower vendors. Stroke a kitten or a squirrel and try your best not to take one home.

Quai de la Mégisserie: 75001, between the Pont au Change and the Pont Neuf. Métro: Châtelet. Open: shop hours vary; most open Mon to Sat 10 am to 6:30 pm.

Phares Point

Debate the meaning of life at **Café des Phares**, a *philocafé* where mixing philosophy with caffeine results in rollicking debates. The *philocafé* concept originated here with owner Marc Sautet and has since spread to over 100 cafés in France alone.

Discussing everything from Santa Claus to sex, the two-hundred-strong group includes students, tourists and residents. Even if you can't speak French, take a look to see French intellectuals at their finest.

If you're itching to jump in, go to the Café de Flore, where an English *philocafé* is held on the first Wednesday of every month.

Café des Phares: 7 Parc de la Place Bastille, 75004, +33 1 42 72 04 70. Métro: Bastille. Café open Sun to Thurs 7 am to 3 am; Fri, Sat 7 am to 4 am. Café Philo held every Sun 11 am to 1 pm. www.cafe-philo-des-phares.info ⏳ 🍸

Café de Flore: 172 Boulevard Saint-Germain, 75006, +33 1 45 48 55 26. Métro: St-Germain-des-Prés. Café open daily 7 am to 2 am. Café Philo held first Wed of every month 7 pm to 9 pm. Check web for details. www.cafe-de-flore.com; www.meetup.com/english-cafe-philo-in-paris 🍸

The Original Goth

Catch a glimpse of the first Gothic building ever built at the **Basilica of Saint Denis**. The final resting place for all but three of France's kings from the tenth to the eighteenth centuries, a place of worship has been on this site since the seventh century.

In the 1100s, Abbot Suger decided to give the building a facelift. Using a variety of trendy new styles – from the pointed arch to the flying buttress – Suger created a template for future Goth builders to follow. In true Gothic (and gory) style, the mummified heart of ten-year-old Louis XVII was later sealed into the wall near the grave of his mother, Marie Antoinette. Leave the tourists behind at Notre Dame and head north to uncover your inner Goth.

Basilique Cathédrale Saint-Denis: 1 Rue de la Légion d'Honneur, 93200, +33 1 48 09 83 54. Métro: Basilique de Saint-Denis. Open: April to Sept, Mon to Sat 10 am to 6:15 pm, Sun 12 pm to 6:15 pm; Oct to Mar, Mon to Sat 10 am to 5 pm, Sun 12 pm to 5:15 pm. Price: adults €7, free for under 18s. http://saint-denis.monuments-nationaux.fr

Credit Crunch Munch

Want some macarons but don't want to pay a fortune? Go to discount store **Monoprix**, where you can get your sugar fix for a fraction of the price. Bite into some pistachio, chocolate, raspberry and cappuccino goo for less than a fiver. It might not be good for your teeth but it's great for your budget.

Monoprix: 9 Boulevard de la Madeleine, 75001, +33 1 42 86 61 54. Métro: Madeleine. Open: Mon to Sat 9 am to 10 pm. Price: Pack of 12 assorted flavours for €4.95. Also other branches. www.monoprix.fr 🛴 👫

Art History

Examine the rich cultural past of Paris' Jewish communities at the **Museum of Jewish Art and History**. Located in the Marais, the building itself – the grand Hôtel de Saint-Aignan – is on the sadder side of history: it is here that the building's Jewish residents were rounded up during the Nazi occupation of France, with thirteen of them dying in concentration camps. Learn about the former inhabitants; see a Torah scroll from the sixteenth century; and read all about the legendary Dreyfus affair, a political scandal involving a Jewish captain that rocked France in the early twentieth century.

Musée d'Art et d'Histoire du Judaïsme: Hôtel de Saint-Aignan, 71 Rue du Temple, 75003, +33 1 53 01 86 60. Métro: Rambuteau, Hôtel de Ville. Open: Mon to Fri 11 am to 6 pm; Sun 10 am to 6 pm. Closed Jewish holidays. Price: €6.80. www.mahj.org

Blonde Ambition

Do blondes really have more fun? Find out at colour legend **Christophe Robin**'s salon. With a bevy of celebrity clients – including Catherine Deneuve and Kristin Scott Thomas – and a wealth of colouring experience, you can bet you're in safe hands. The first to open a salon dedicated to colour and the care of hair, Robin's luxurious new set-up at the Meurice will soothe your soul, too. Stretch out, get a manicure at the same time, and let the bleach take hold.

Christophe Robin: The Salon at the Meurice, Suite 128-129, 228 Rue de Rivoli, 75001, +33 1 40 20 02 83. Métro: Tuileries. Open: Mon to Fri 10 am to 7 pm. www.colorist.net

Make Good

Press the button under the plaque, push open the heavy wooden door and you'll be admitted to the inner sanctum of the art world. Opened in 1995 – roughly 20 years after its counterpart in New York City – the **Marian Goodman Gallery** has exhibited influential artists like Gerhard Richter and Steve McQueen. Dive in and nose around one of Paris' best-loved galleries.

Marian Goodman: 79 Rue du Temple, 75003, +33 1 48 04 70 52. Métro: Rambuteau. Open: Tues to Sat 11 am to 7 pm. Price: free. www.mariangoodman.com

Because You're Worth It

Who says men can't have facials – or even a bit of Botox? Certainly not Philippe Dumont, whose **Nickel Spa** caters exclusively to the needs of the modern man, offering treatments to reduce your love handles or stay tanned all year round. With its metallic looking products and almost clinical surroundings, the Nickel Spa can make a beauty believer out of even the most cynical male. And you may just run into John Malkovich or Jean Paul Gaultier, reputed to be regulars here.

Nickel Spa: 48 Rue des Francs Bourgeois, 75003, +33 1 42 77 41 10. Métro: Hôtel de Ville. Open: Mon, Tues, Fri, Sat 11 am to 7:30 pm; Wed, Thurs 11 am to 9 pm. www.nickel.fr

All Dolled Up

If you haven't outgrown your childhood desire for dolls, you can more than satisfy your craving at the **Doll Museum**. With over five hundred dolls made from materials like bisque, cloth and rubber, there's plenty to resurrect childhood memories. And if your favourite pal is in need of some tender loving care, there's even a Doll Hospital where you can restore it to its former glory. The museum holds weekly workshops for children on everything from creating miniature doll food to fashioning an outfit for the legendary Barbie. Want one to go? Choose a new treasure from the doll store on site.

La Musée de la Poupée: Impasse Berthaud, 75003, +33 1 42 72 73 11. Métro: Rambuteau. Open: Tues to Sun 10 am to 6 pm. Price: adult €8; student 12 to 25 €5; child 3 to 11 €3. www.museedelapoupeeparis.com 🕴

Kahn Do

He was a man of great ambition: to capture humans from across the globe using colour photography. Nowadays, that doesn't seem too lofty. But back in Albert Kahn's time – the start of the twentieth century – such technology was still in its infancy. Hoping his project would create world peace, the wealthy Kahn sent more than fifty photographers around the world, from Vietnam to Norway. From 1909 to 1931, they snapped 72,000 autochromes of a world in flux: from the last Celtic villages in Ireland to the collapse of the Austro-Hungarian empire.

Located at Kahn's former residence, the **Albert Kahn Museum** displays what Kahn called 'The Archives of the Planet'. Kahn's philosophy of bringing the world together is also evident in his garden, which consists of Japanese, French, English and even African wildlife.

Take a stroll around the world and see the past in living colour.

Musée Albert Kahn: 10-14 Rue du Port, 92100, +33 1 55 19 28 00, Boulogne-Billancourt. Métro: Boulogne-Pont de Saint Cloud. Open: Tues to Sun 11 am to 7 pm (May to Sept); 11 am to 6 pm (rest of the year). Price: €1.50. www.albertkahn.co.uk/museum.html; www.albert-kahn.fr

Clock Watch

Browse some Degas, then sit back and watch time tick away as you dine behind the giant clock at the **Musée d'Orsay**. Located in the Gare d'Orsay, a former railway station built between 1898 and 1900, the museum exhibits works of art from 1848 to 1915. Sate your artistic appetite by taking in the world's largest collection of impressionist paintings from Monet to Manet and Cézanne to Renoir. Then satisfy your baser needs at the Café des Hauteurs where you can grab a gourmet sandwich with time on your side.

Musée d'Orsay: 62 Rue de Lille, 75007, +33 1 40 49 48 14. Métro: Solférino. Open: Tues to Sun 9:30 am to 6 pm; open until 9:30 pm on Thursdays. Café open Tues to Sun 10 am to 5 pm; Thurs from 10:30 am to 9 pm. Price: €8; concessions €5.50. www.musee-orsay.fr

Simply Chic

Parisians' simple yet chic attire is legendary. To emulate that effortless style, head straight to *Atelier de Production et de Création*, otherwise known as **A.P.C.** Founded in 1988 by Tunisian-born designer Jean Touitou, the brand aims to revolt against everything pretentious. The shops are equally low-key – you might walk right by one if you weren't looking for it. If you can't find the perfect minimalist garment, take away a custom-made A.P.C. compact disc to fuel your retail dreams at home.

A.P.C.: 38 Rue Madame, 75006, +33 1 42 22 12 77. Métro: Saint-Sulpice. Open: Mon to Sat 11 am to 7 pm. www.apc.fr

Monet's the Man

You can never have too much of a good thing and **Musée Marmottan Monet** – with the largest collection of Monet paintings in the world – more than proves the point. Fill your eyes with Monet's creations and see where it all began with the very painting for which the Impressionist movement was named (*Impression Soleil Levant*). If you can tear yourself away from the main event, check out the other artworks by Monet's contemporaries, including Renoir and Manet.

Musée Marmottan Monet: 2 Rue Louis-Boilly, 75016, +33 1 44 96 50 33. Métro: Muette. Open: Tues to Sun 11 am to 6 pm; until 9 pm on Tues. Price: €9; students under 25 €5. www.marmottan.com

Get Shirty

Make like a deity and conjure up divine creations at tailor **Eglé Bespoke**. *Eglé* means goddess in Greek, and you'll certainly feel invincible with so much creative power at your fingertips. Choose from over 2,500 fabrics, customise your shirt with embroidery and even get your own mantra engraved on your buttons.

At this tailor, anything is possible.

Eglé Bespoke: 26 Rue du Mont Thabor, 75001, +33 1 44 15 98 31. Métro: Concorde. Open: Mon to Sat 11 am to 7 pm. www.eglebespoke.com

Sewer Rat

Head for the tunnels – sewer tunnels, that is – in one of the city's quirkiest museums, the **Paris Sewer Museum**. Paris has had a basic sewer system since the thirteenth century, when sewers drained wastewater into the Seine. The current sewer system was designed in 1850, with large underground pipes for carrying off waste and a separate system for drinking water. Since then, hundreds of kilometres of sewer tunnels have been added.

Enter the subterranean maze, learn about its history and development, and follow the streets above from underground (street signs in the sewers will let you know exactly where you are). You can even see which house the pipes are leading up to – each spout carries a number matching the street above. Gain a new appreciation (or disgust) for what's down below.

Musée des Egouts de Paris: Place de la Résistance (93 Quai d'Orsay), Pont de l'Alma, 75007, +33 1 47 05 10 29. Métro: Alma-Marceau. Open: Sat to Wed 11 am to 5 pm (summer); 11 am to 4 pm (winter). Price: adults €4.20, children €3.40. Closed last 3 weeks of Jan. www.egouts.tenebres.eu 🚹🚺

Write Stuff

It won't be a chore to write a letter home with all the beautiful pens and paper on offer at **Cassegrain.** Open since 1919, this shop has engraved copper plates for legends like Churchill and de Gaulle, as well as providing less venerable customers with a wide selection of writing utensils and notebooks. Practise your cursive and order up some personalised stationery.

Cassegrain: 422 Rue Saint-Honoré, 75008, +33 1 42 60 20 08. Métro: Concorde. Open: Mon to Sat 10 am to 7 pm. www.cassegrain.fr

Mother Lode

Warm up your belly for the lunch ahead with a little bit of sweetness at **À la Mère de Famille.** The sweet shop first opened its doors on this very location in 1761 as Maison Bernard, and through the years it's grown into the vision of candy heaven here today. Grab a truffle or eyeball the wide array of other sweets on show, then pay up at the antique cash register. Adult or child, you can't help acting like a kid in a candy shop here.

À la Mère de Famille: 33-35 Rue du Faubourg Montmartre, 75009, +33 1 47 70 83 69. Métro: Cadet or Le Peletier. Open: Mon to Sat 10 am to 7 pm. www.lameredefamille.com 👫

Let 'er Rip

Visit the Grande Dame of all fabric stores, **Tissus Reine**. A mecca for those who like to fashion their own creations, your imagination will run wild at their four floors of fabrics.

Grab a butterfly notion, a pattern book or a handful of buttons and get your wardrobe all sewn up.

If one fabric shop isn't enough to satisfy you, head to nearby **Marché St Pierre** where the five floors of fabrics should sate your clothing appetite.

Tissus Reine: 3-5 Place St Pierre, 75018, +33 1 46 06 02 31. Métro: Anvers or Abbesses. Open: Mon 2 pm to 6:30 pm; Tues to Fri 9:30 am to 6:30 pm; Sat 9:30 am to 6:45 pm. www.tissus-reine.com

Dreyfus Déballage du Marché Saint Pierre: 2 Rue Charles Nodier, 75018, +33 1 46 06 92 25. Métro: Abbesses, Anvers. Open: Mon to Fri 10 am to 6:30 pm, Sat to 7 pm. www.marchesaintpierre.com

Shop a Block

Paris is renowned for its wide array of shopping choices, but with so much on offer it's hard to know just where to begin! With **Chic Shopping** Paris tours, though, money won't be burning a hole in your pocket for long. Choose from a 'Unique Boutique' tour pilfering goodies from the shops in the Marais, or find items only fashioned in France with the 'Made in France' excursion. Go vintage with the 'Arts and Antiques' tour or find some super sweet duds for your little one on the 'Chic Bébé' outing.

With bilingual guides (who aren't on commission) to help you along your shopping way, you can be sure to exercise a little purchasing power.

Chic Shopping Paris: +33 6 77 65 08 01. Prices and times depend on tour chosen; check website for details. www.chicshoppingparis.com ⌛

Ghost Square

Named in honour of French explorer Samuel de Champlain (who founded Canada's Quebec City in 1608), **Square Samuel de Champlain** is fittingly home to a 150-year-old maple tree. But it's a wall – designed in 1909 in memory of all victims of revolutions – that really catches the eye. Ghostly figures appear to be trapped in stone, unable to break free. Sink down on the grass and lose yourself in the spectral illusion.

Square Samuel de Champlain: 75020. Métro: Père Lachaise or Gambetta. Open: weekdays from 8 am, weekends and holidays from 9 am. Closing times from 5 pm in winter to 9:30 pm in summer. Price: free.

24 Hour Fact

Paris has 12 'super-loos'
open from 6 am to 10 pm.

24 Hours with the Kids

12:00

Cheese Please!

If you've ever yearned to create a match made in heaven between cheese and wine, enrol in **Go Learn To's Wine and Cheese Pairing Course**. Fill your belly with bread and cheese, drink a glass (or five) of wine, and see how much you remember at the end! Never fear if it's all a blur – you can take away a list of the wines and cheeses you've tried.

Wine and Cheese Pairing Course: Rue de Rivoli, 75001. Métro: Louvre-Rivoli. Exact address supplied upon booking. Courses run Mon, Wed, Fri, Sat at 12 pm. Price: £62. www.golearnto.com/course/overview/967/Wine+and+Cheese+Pairing+Course ⌛

Pigeon Proof

Forego the graves of Jean-Paul Sartre, Simone de Beauvoir and other artistic notables buried in **Montparnasse Cemetery** and head straight for the strangest grave of them all: that of inventor Charles Pigeon, whose stone form lies beside his wife in a full-sized bed atop the family tomb. He's not indulging in some after-life hanky-panky, though: both he and his wife are fully dressed (and under the watchful gaze of a guardian angel). Pigeon, who died in 1915, made his fortune by inventing a non-exploding gasoline lamp. Notebook in hand, he's still set to capture his future ideas for all of eternity.

Cimetière Montparnasse: 3 Boulevard Edgard Quinet, 75014. Métro: Raspail. Open: Nov to Mar, Mon to Fri 8 am to 5:30 pm, Sat 8:30 am to 5:30 pm, Sun 9 am to 5:30 pm; April to Oct, Mon to Fri 8 am to 6 pm, Sat 8:30 am to 6 pm, Sun 9 am to 6 pm. Maps available from guards. www.pariscemeteries.com

The Business of Eating

Dine under the sun or the stars at **Le Café du Commerce**, where the sliding roof and plant-lined balconies make it feel like an al fresco experience. Located in a former fabric shop, owners Marie and Etienne Guerraud take their steak (from Limousin) and frites (from Flanders) very seriously. Try a little of the legendary egg mayo, suck back an oyster or two, and enjoy a truly Parisian dining experience.

Le Café du Commerce: 51 Rue Commerce, 75015, +33 1 45 75 03 27. Métro: Avenue Emile Zola, Cambronne, Commerce. Open: daily 12 pm to 3 pm, 7 pm to 12 am. www.lecafeducommerce.com 🍗

Ray of Light

Originally built to house Louis IX's relics of Christ, **Sainte-Chapelle** is now known for its stained glass, two-thirds of which is original. The chapel is considered to be an outstanding example of the *rayonnant* style of Gothic architecture, when designers tried to flood buildings with light. Go when it's sunny and watch the coloured light stream through the Rose Window. With every stained glass window depicting a different story, it's possible to stare for hours if your eyes can stand it.

Sainte-Chapelle: 4 Boulevard du Palais, 75001 +33 1 53 40 60 80. Métro: Cité. Open: daily (summer) 9:30 am to 6 pm; (winter) 9 am to 5 pm. Price: €8, concessions €5. http://sainte-chapelle.monuments-nationaux.fr

Hats Off

Napoléon and his hat parted ways at **Café Procope**, said to be Paris' first café. The young officer couldn't pay for his meal and his beloved hat was left as collateral. It's still there today, displayed proudly behind glass. Founded in 1686, Procope attracted everyone from Voltaire to Robespierre, all there for the drink of the hour: coffee. Just make sure you can pay the bill or you might lose your hat, too!

Café Procope: 13 Rue de l'Ancienne Comédie, 75006, +33 1 40 46 79 00. Métro: Odéon. Open daily 10:30 am to 1 am. www.procope.com 🦟

Pant Up the Panthéon

There's no lift, so if you want to climb to the top of the **Panthéon** you'll have to do it the hard way: under your own steam-power. It's worth it, though, for the remarkable 360 degree view from this imposing structure atop Sainte-Geneviève Mountain. Completed in 1790 as a church dedicated to Sainte Geneviève, it was decreed as the place to bury great Frenchmen after the French Revolution. Jean-Jacques Rousseau and Victor Hugo are both interred in the necropolis here. Check out their tombs, then head to the top of the great dome (only with a guide, from April to October). Catch your breath and take in the city spread out before you.

Le Panthéon: Place du Panthéon, 75005, +33 1 44 32 18 00. Métro: Cardinale Lemoine. Open: Apr to Sept daily 10 am to 6:30 pm, Oct to March daily 10 am to 6 pm. Dome open only from Apr to Oct. Price: €8; €5 concessions. http://pantheon.monuments-nationaux.fr

Tea and Toast

If your French isn't quite up to literary level and you want some good reading material, head to **Tea and Tattered Pages** where their shelves of second-hand English books will make you feel right at home. Push your way through the stacks towards the back of the shop, where you'll find a cosy café. Wrap your hands around a mug of English tea, chomp on some cinnamon toast, and you'll be ready to face the French world once again.

Tea and Tattered Pages: 24 Rue Mayet, 75006, +33 1 40 65 94 35. Métro: Duroc. Open: Mon to Sat 11 am to 7 pm; Sun 12 pm to 6 pm. www.teaandtatteredpages.com

Eggsperts

Devoted to the humble egg, restaurant **Coco & Co** dresses them up in so many ways you'll hardly recognise them. From caviar and foie gras omelettes to the *cocotte* burger, eggs have never had it so good.

Cosy yet chic, make sure to book if you don't want to wait.

Coco & Co: 11 Rue de Bernard Pallissy, 75006, +33 1 45 44 02 52. Métro: Saint-Germain-des-Prés. Open for lunch and dinner Wed to Fri; 12 pm to 4:30 pm Sat, Sun. www.cocoandco.fr ⚱️🍴

Go for Guerlain

Get gorgeous at the headquarters of famous luxury *parfumier* **Guerlain** as you watch the minions scurry below on the Champs-Elysées. Opened in 1939, the Guerlain Institute has undergone a multi-million Euro revamp by famous French interior designer Andrée Putman. Decked out in luxurious white and gold, you'll feel like royalty – and look like one, too – after choosing from their long list of treatments, including facials using orchid extracts to make your skin look fresher. Finish it off with a squirt of their heady perfume.

L'Institut Guerlain: 68 Avenue des Champs Elysées, 75008, +33 1 45 62 11 21. Métro: George V or Franklin D. Roosevelt. Open: Mon to Sat 9:30 am to 6:45 pm. www.guerlainspa.com

Darwin Drama

Science comes alive at the **Grande Galerie d'Évolution**, located in the Jardin des Plantes. Aimed at explaining Darwin's theory to the younger generation, adults will be fascinated too as they take in the life-sized animals marching two by two through the centuries; the reconstruction of a giant squid; or the extinct species room. With over seven thousand specimens, there's something to interest everyone.

And if you want to look at some live animals, head to the nearby **Ménagerie** where a zoo of more than 13 acres and a variety of birds, mammals and reptiles awaits.

Grande Galerie d'Evolution: Jardin des Plantes, 36 Rue Geoffroy-Saint-Hilaire, 75005, +33 1 40 79 56 01. Métro: Gare d'Austerlitz or Jussieu. Open: daily (except Tuesdays) 10 am to 6 pm. Price: Grande Galerie €9, concessions €7.

Ménagerie: Rue Geoffroy-Saint-Hilaire, Place Valhubert, 75005, +33 1 40 79 37 94. Métro: Gare d'Austerlitz or Jussieu. Open: daily 9 am to 6 pm; until 6:30 pm Sun. Price: €8, concessions €6. 🕴

Crêpe Expectations

The crêpe may have its roots in Brittany, but it's the stuff of legends at **Chez Josselin**. Located close to the Montparnasse train station (with a direct train to Brittany), this tiny crêperie is nestled amongst a whole host of other restaurants selling the national dish. Bretons coming to Paris for work settled around the train station, and restaurants set up shop to serve their crêpe cravings. The best of the bunch, Chez Josselin is cosy, cluttered and fast! Choose a dinner crêpe (with savoury filling, called *galette*) or satisfy your sweet-tooth with a traditional sugar crêpe. Either way, you can't go wrong at Chez Josselin.

Chez Josselin: 67 Rue du Montparnasse, 75014, +33 1 43 20 93 50. Métro: Edgar Quinet or Montparnasse. Open: Tues to Sun 12 pm to 11 pm. 🦐

Out of Africa

Rough and ready, the market at **Place d'Aligre** is where to go for some North African spice along with your daily groceries. The market consists of two parts: the food-based Marché Beauvau, one of the few surviving covered markets in Paris, and the flea market outside where stall owners aggressively flog books, fabrics and assorted bric-a-brac. Make sure not to miss the Rue d'Aligre, where the North African character of the area really shows with shops selling everything from sweet honey-dipped pastries to melons.

If all the pushing and shoving has tired you out, head to nearby **Le Baron Bouge**, where you can grab a plate of oysters, a glass of wine directly from one of the numerous barrels scattered about, and rest your feet (if you can find a seat!).

Marche d'Aligre: between Rue du Faubourg Saint-Antoine and Rue de Charenton. Métro: Ledru-Rollin. Open: daily (except Mon). Stall owners usually pack up by 1 pm; 2 pm on Sun. Best bargains found on Sun before closing. Shops on street have regular hours. http://marchedaligre.free.fr

Le Baron Bouge: 1 Rue Théophile Roussel, 75012, +33 1 43 43 14 32. Métro: Ledru-Rollin. Open: Tues to Fri 10 am to 2 pm; 5 pm to 10 pm. ⧖ 🍽

Stuff It

Fancy a stuffed bird? How about a zebra? If you've always wanted a little bit of taxidermy to decorate your house, you can get it at **Deyrolle**. Founded in 1831, Deyrolle's mission is to increase human understanding of nature through observation – even if the nature isn't actually still alive. In February 2008, a fire damaged the store's legendary Cabinets of Curiosities along with its historical collections, but recovery is underway and Deyrolle has re-opened to the public. Browse the collection of snake skeletons, shells and butterflies, all under the beady eye of a giant giraffe.

If you have the desire – and the cash – you can even take one home.

Deyrolle: 46 Rue du Bac, 75007, +33 1 42 22 30 07. Métro: Rue du Bac. Open: Mon 10 am to 1 pm, 2 pm to 7 pm; Tues to Fri 10 am to 7 pm. www.deyrolle.fr ⌛ 👫

Urban Living

For Swiss-born architect Le Corbusier, the urban age demanded a new style of architecture and his Modular system – creating houses from interconnecting rectangles arranged just so – more than hit the mark. Get inside the mind of an architectural genius at **Fondation Le Corbusier**, said to hold the largest collection of Le Corbusier drawings in the world.

Located in Maison La Roche, a house built in 1923 as one of Le Corbusier's earliest Paris commissions, you can see over 8,000 of the architect's drawings and plans. Just don't expect to find any sofas to sit on: for Le Corbusier, 'chairs are architecture, sofas are bourgeois.'

Fondation Le Corbusier: 8-10 Square du Docteur Blanche, 75016, +33 1 42 88 41 53. Métro: Jasmin, Michel-Ange-Autieul. Library (by appointment): Mon to Thurs 1:30 pm to 6 pm; Friday 1:30 pm to 5 pm. Maison La Roche open Mon 1:30 pm to 6 pm; Tues to Thurs 10 am to 6 pm; Fri and Sat 10 am to 5 pm. Price: €4. www.fondationlecorbusier.asso.fr

Buddha Breather

Need some air? Head to Paris' lung, the **Bois de Vincennes**, for a break with Buddha. Located on the edge of Lac Daumesnil, the **Pagode de Vincennes** features the largest Buddha statue in Europe. Take a deep breath in and try to relax under this nine-metre-high statue, covered in gold leaf. Built in 1931 as part of the French Colonial Exposition, the pagoda is now used as a place of worship for Paris' Buddhist community. Even if you don't need to recharge your batteries, the Bois de Vincennes is worth a visit in itself. Three times the size of Central Park, this park has everything from a fairy-tale chateau to a horse-racing track, a zoo, and even a school for wayward dogs!

Pagode de Vincennes: Route de la Ceinture du Lac Dausmenil, 75012, +33 1 40 04 98 06. Métro: Porte Dorée. Open: as below. www.kagyudzong.org

Bois de Vincennes: Avenue de Paris, 75012, +33 1 43 28 41 59. Métro: Château de Vincennes, Porte Dorée, Porte de Charenton. Open: daily, times vary by sunset. www.jardins.paris.fr 🛉🛉

Pretty Crafty

It may seem incongruous to house a museum dedicated to science and technology in an old abbey, but that's exactly the contradiction you'll encounter at the **Museum of Arts and Crafts**. Its exhibits range from ancient scientific instruments, including astrological and laboratory equipment, to modern-day materials like plastics. And you can't help but be impressed by the original Foucault pendulum, an experiment designed to measure the rotation of the earth.

Musée des Arts et Métiers: 60 Rue Réaumur, 75003, +33 1 53 01 82 00. Métro: Arts et Métiers. Open: Tues to Sun 10 am to 6 pm; to 9:30 pm on Thurs. Price: adults €6.50, free for under 18s. www.arts-et-metiers.net

White Out

It's not your ordinary dishware: at **Astier de Villatte**, crockery takes on a whole new meaning. Fashioned from gleaming white ceramic, you can fill your kitchen with plates cut like stars and frivolously frilly tea-cups. Designed by Parisian artist Nathalie Lété – whose inspiration is vintage toys and old engravings – dining will never be the same again.

Astier de Villatte: 173 Rue St Honoré, 75001 +33 1 42 60 74 13. Métro: Palais Royal-Musée du Louvre. Open: Mon to Sat 11 am to 7:30 pm. www.astierdevillatte.com

Sea History

If your land legs are weary, sail over to the Palais de Chaillot for the **National Museum of the Marine**. One of the oldest nautical museums in the world, you can learn about all things sea-related, from Jules Verne to the latest research vessels. See Napoléon's ornate barge, peer inside a metal diving suit from 1882 and check out Océan – a ship from the 1800s with 120 cannons – for some real sea-power.

Musée Nationale de la Marine: Palais de Chaillot, 17 Place du Trocadéro, 75116, +33 1 53 65 69 69. Métro: Trocadéro. Open: daily (except Tues) 10 am to 6 pm. Price: €7; concessions €5; free for under 18s. www.musee-marine.fr 👫

Pig Paradise

They may be just another fungus, but when it comes to cuisine truffles are worth their weight in gold. Known as the 'diamonds of the kitchen', you can sniff your way to paradise at truffle heaven **Maison de la Truffe**. Open since 1932, the shop sells everything from truffle-infused olive oil to vinegar with truffle slivers. Have a seat in the elegant tasting room and fill your belly with the truffle-laden menu. Takeaway or sit down, it's all truffle here, all the time.

Maison de la Truffe: 19 Place de la Madeleine, 75008, +33 1 42 65 53 22. Métro: Madeleine. Open: Mon to Sat 12 pm to 10:30 pm (tasting room open from 12 pm). www.maison-de-la-truffe.fr 🍄

Tower Power

Deemed by many as a blight on Paris' skyline, Parisians often say the view from **Montparnasse Tower** is the most beautiful in Paris, for one reason: it's the only place where you can't see it! At 210 metres and with 59 floors, the tallest building in France is unavoidable from almost any other vantage point.

Take the high-speed lift – only 38 seconds – to the fifty-sixth floor and enjoy the 360-degree views over the city below. Munch a sandwich while taking in the Sacré Coeur or zoom in to the sights with the binoculars. Whichever direction you choose to look, you're guaranteed some spectacular sights.

Montparnasse Tower: 33 Avenue du Maine, 75015, +33 1 45 38 52 56. Métro: Edgar Quinet. Open: Apr 1 to Sept 30, daily 9:30 am to 11:30 pm (last lift at 11 pm). Oct 1 to Mar 31, Sun to Thurs 9:30 am to 10:30 pm; Fri, Sat and day before a bank holiday 9:30 am to 11 pm (last lift 30 mins before closing). Café open daily for lunch and dinner. Price: adults €11; students (16 to 20) €8; children (7 to 15) €4.70; children 6 and under free. www.tourmontparnasse56.com 🎥 👫

Little India

Spice things up at **Passage Brady**, located between Rue du Faubourg Saint-Denis and Rue du Faubourg Saint-Martin. Indian restaurants, spice shops and, oddly, barber shops line this 218-metre-long covered arcade. While it's miles from its posh cousins in wealthier neighbourhoods, it's just as chock full of delights. Grab a Bollywood DVD to practise your dance moves, get spruced up with a trim, then sit down at **Pooja** for some North Indian grub and a taste of the exotic without leaving the city.

Passage Brady: between Rue du Faubourg Saint-Denis and Rue du Faubourg Saint-Martin, 75010. Métro: Château d'Eau or Strasbourg-Saint-Denis.

Pooja: 91 Passage Brady, 75010, +33 1 48 24 00 83. Métro: Château d'Eau or Strasbourg-Saint-Denis. Open: daily 12 pm to 3 pm; 7 pm to 11 pm. 🎥

13:00

Fork Out

If money is no object and you're looking for the ultimate Parisian brunch, hit the oldest **Ritz** in the world. For just over €100 you can eat your eggs (and so much more) at the hotel's restaurant L'Espadon, which earned a coveted Michelin star in 2007. Listen to the live piano, send the little ones off to the games area (with marshmallows on offer, they'll be sure to go willingly) and head out to the lush garden. And if all that food has made you sleepy, you can also reserve a room – starting from the mere price of around €550 per night.

The Ritz: 15 Place Vendôme, 75001, +33 1 43 16 30 80 (for reservations). Brunch 11 am to 3 pm every Sun. Price: €115 (excluding drinks). Métro: Opéra, Madeleine. www.ritzparis.com ⌛🍴

Gallery of agnès b.

Better known for her clothing designs, inside agnès b.'s stark-white **Galerie du Jour** is some serious art. Founded in 1984, the gallery has exhibited artists like Gilbert & George and has played a unique role in fostering the acceptance of street art. Drop in and see a whole other side to the French fashion legend.

Galerie du Jour: 44 Rue Quincampoix, 75004, +33 1 44 54 55 90. Métro: Rambuteau. Open: Tues to Sat 12 pm to 7 pm. Price: free. www.galeriedujour.com

Go for a Spin

Let all the sights blur into one as you take a ride on the carousel at the **Tuileries Gardens**. Designed in 1664 by famous landscaper André Le Nôtre, the area used to be a clay pit for making tiles (in French, *tuilerie*). Now, it covers 54 hectares of prime land. Its central location makes it a popular place for Parisians to stroll between the sculptures which pepper the grounds, and for young ones to hit the funfair, ride donkeys and even get their hands dirty with some gardening of their own.

Once you're done with the great outdoors, head over to nearby **Angelina** where you can warm your hands with a cup of creamy hot chocolate or a spot of tea. Opened in 1903, this tearoom has been visited in the past by Coco Chanel, Marcel and Proust. Add your name to the list and succumb to Angelina's charms.

Jardin des Tuileries: Place de la Concorde, 75001. Métro: Tuileries or Concorde. Open: daily, April to May 7 am to 9 pm; Jun to Aug 7 am to 11 pm; Sept to March 7:30 am to 7:30 pm. Funfair and children's activities held July and Aug. ⌛ 👫

Angelina: 226 Rue de Rivoli, 75001, +33 1 42 60 82 00. Métro: Tuileries. Open: daily 9 am to 7 pm. www.groupe-bertrand.com 🍴

A Dog's Death

Dogs live a gilded life in Paris, with their own grooming salons, designer fashions and even their own plates in restaurants. So it makes sense that in death, too, they have their own dedicated burial ground. If you want to pay homage to some French fidos, take a trip to the **Dog Cemetery**. Thought to be the oldest pet cemetery in the world, it's home to canine heroes like Barry, a St Bernard mountain rescue dog who saved over forty people. Hollywood stars like Rin Tin Tin are also resting in peace, alongside a menagerie of other worthy animals including horses and fish.

Cimetière des Chiens: 4 Pont de Clichy, Île des Ravageurs, Asnières-sur-Seine, 92600. Métro: Gabriel Péri, then a 15-minute walk. Open: daily (except Mon) 10 am to 6 pm (until 4:30 pm in winter). Price: adults €3; children age 6 to 11 €1; under 6s free. 🚹

Sandwich Artists

You may wonder why on earth you'd eat a Vietnamese sandwich – otherwise known as *bánh mì* – in Paris, but one bite of this meat and veggie combo topped with spicy sauce and you'll wonder how you lived without it. Ever since legendary food blogger Clotilde Dusoulier raved about **Saigon Sandwich**, Parisians and tourists alike have flocked to the hole-in-the-wall for their fix. Choose from three sandwich options, squeeze into one of the few chairs available or head for nearby Belleville Park. Either way, your taste buds will thank you.

Saigon Sandwich: 8 Rue de la Présentation, 75011. Métro: Belleville. Open: Mon to Sat 10 am to 6 pm; Sun 10 am to 2 pm. 🦞

No Strings Attached

Get out in the open and rid yourself of any technological constraints with free wireless access at the **Arènes de Lutèce**. This amphitheatre was built by the Romans in the first century and was initially used as a theatre, sporting venue and circus. Discovered in the 1860s when nearby Rue Monge was constructed, the arena was restored thanks to the support of the artistic community of the time, including Victor Hugo. Now, you can take advantage of modern-day technology as you browse for your favourite Romans. And if you tire of your laptop, why not take to the arena for a game of *boules*?

Square des Arènes de Lutèce: 47 Rue Monge, 75005. Métro: Place Monge, Cardinal Lemoine, Jussieu. Open: daily 8 am to 5:45 pm (winter); until 9:30 pm (summer). Open from 9 am on weekends and holidays. Price: entry free; wireless access free.

Food Therapy

You can't buy medicine anymore at this old pharmacy, but hanging out in the quirky restaurant combined with a cosy bookstore is like a balm for your soul. Order some vegetarian grub, gulp hot chocolate or organic tea, browse the books and let the calm of **La Pharmacie** restore you.

La Pharmacie: 22 Rue Jean-Pierre Timbaud, 75011, +33 1 55 28 75 98. Métro: Oberkampf. Open: daily 12 pm to 11 pm. 🍸

All About Paris

Get a large helping of Paris history at the **Carnavalet Museum**, dedicated to all things Paris. Housed in two imposing mansions in the Marais – with over 20,000 drawings, 150,000 photos and 800 pieces of furniture – you can be sure to get a well-rounded view of Paris' past from ancient settlement to urban centre. See paintings of Madame de Sévigné, once thought to be Paris' most beautiful woman; Marie-Antoinette's personal belongings; and the cradle of Napoléon's son. The museum offers up Paris on a plate, and you can't help but devour it.

Musée Carnavalet: Hôtel Carnavalet, 23 Rue de Sévigné, 75003, +33 1 44 59 58 58. Métro: Chemin Vert or Saint Paul. Open: daily (except Mon and holidays) 10 am to 6 pm. Price: free, unless for special exhibitions or conferences. www.carnavalet.paris.fr

Libation Inspiration

Looking for the place where artists hang out? Head to **La Palette**, where you might meet a Monet in the making. Students and teachers from the nearby fine arts school go here for its old-school charm – not much has changed (except the prices!) since the interior was decorated in 1935. The waiters are renowned for their brusqueness but don't let that put you off; it's as much a part of the La Palette experience as the battle for a spot on the sprawling terrace.

La Palette: 43 Rue de Seine, 75006, +33 1 43 26 68 15. Métro: Saint-Germain-des-Prés. Café and bar open Mon to Sat 9 am to 2 am; restaurant open Mon to Sat 11:30 am to 3 pm. Closed in August. 🍷

Unicorn Porn

They may only exist in fairy-tales but the six unicorn tapestries at the **Musée de Cluny** – made famous by Tracy Chevalier's novel *The Lady and the Unicorn* – are almost as good as the real thing. Each depicting a woman and a unicorn, five of the tapestries are named after the senses with the sixth entitled *A Mon Seul Désire* (To My Only Desire). Interpretations vary, but it is commonly thought the series portrays a virgin seducing a unicorn, based on the myth that unicorns are so wild only virgins can tame them.

Whatever the tapestries are meant to represent, they are considered to be one of the greatest art works of the European Middle Ages. You can make up your own mind and browse everything from Gothic sculpture to the everyday items of the Middle-Aged man.

Musée de Cluny (National Museum of the Middle Ages – The Baths and Hôtel de Cluny): 6 Place Paul Painlevé, 75005, +33 1 53 73 78 00. Métro: Cluny-La Sorbonne, Saint-Michel or Odéon. Open: daily (except Tues) 9:15 am to 5:45 pm. Price: €8.50; for 18 to 25s €6.50; free for under 26s who are EU citizens. www.musee-moyenage.fr

MARSHA MOORE   13:00

Get Lucky

Rest your weary feet at **Au Petit Fer à Cheval** – the little horseshoe – and have a glass or two at the horseshoe-shaped bar while you await your second wind. In the centre of the shopping paradise that is the Marais, it's the ideal place to get a quick bite and top up your luck before you hit the streets again. If you can't get a seat at the bar, take your chances on the terrace. Wherever you sit, make sure to check out the gleaming Jules-Verne-themed toilets.

Au Petit Fer à Cheval: 30 Rue Vieille du Temple, 75004, + 33 1 42 72 47 47. Métro: Hôtel de Ville, Saint-Paul. Open: Mon to Sun 9 am to 2 am.

Big MAC

Get away from Monet at the **Museum of Contemporary Art at Val du Marne** (better known as MAC/VAL). Dedicated to art from the 1950s onwards and housed in a stark-white modern building, you couldn't be further from the old Masters if you tried. Opened in 1995 to bring art to the Parisian suburbs, you can see works by French artists Annette Messager and Arman; check out the 150-seat cinema for avant-garde dance and video; browse the bookstore to learn more about your favourite artist; and grab a bite in the restaurant.

And if you need to clear your head, stroll around the open-air exhibition in the large gardens outside. With a constantly evolving programme showcasing emerging French artists, you can be sure you'll never be stuck in the past here.

76

Musée d'Art Contemporain du Val de Marne (MAC/VAL): Place de la Libération, 94400, Vitry-sur-Seine, +33 1 43 91 64 20. Métro: line 7 (direction Mairie d'Ivry) or tramway T3 to Porte de Choisy, then bus 183. Stop: Mac Museum-Val. Open: Tue to Sun 12 pm to 7 pm. Price: €5, concessions €2.50. Free admission first Sun of each month. www.macval.fr

Mosque Meal

You may not think of a mosque as a place to bathe and eat, but at the **Paris Mosque** you can do both in stunning surroundings. The largest mosque in France, it was built after World War I to thank North African Muslims for their contribution to the war effort. Get a guided tour, hit the Turkish baths (with separate days for men and women) and take some mint tea and tagine all in one go. Surrounded by flowers and fountains in a quiet courtyard – with a thirty-three-metre-high minaret looking down – it's hard to believe you're still in Paris.

Grande Mosquée de Paris: 39 Rue Geoffroy-Saint-Hilaire, Place du Puits-de-l'Ermite, 75005, +33 1 43 31 38 20. Métro: Place Monge, Saint Marcel. Mosque open Sat to Thurs 9 am to 12 pm, 2 pm to 6 pm. ⌛ 🦞

Tearoom open daily 9 am to 11:30 pm. Restaurant open daily 12 pm to 3 pm, 7 pm to 10:30 pm. Hammam open for women Mon, Wed, Thurs, Sat 10 am to 9 pm; Fri 2 pm to 9 pm. Men: Tues 2 pm to 9 pm; Sun 10 am to 9 pm. Price: €3 for entry to mosque. Hammam €15. www.la-mosquee.com

High Life

Get a taste of the aristocratic life at the **Museum of Nissim de Camondo**. Wealthy Parisian banker Moïse de Camondo amassed a vast collection of French furniture and art from the eighteenth century. Eager to share his store, he built a luxurious mansion with the intention of passing on both collection and building to his son, Nissim. Sadly Nissim died in an air battle during World War I, and Moïse's daughter and her family perished in the Nazi camps. The Camondo legacy lives on, though, through the perfectly preserved mansion providing a glimpse into the high life.

Glide among the ornate furniture, gilded clocks, intricate tapestries and crystal chandeliers, and you'll feel like you've been transported into a different world.

Musée Nissim de Camondo: 63 Rue de Monceau, 75008, +33 1 53 89 06 50. Métro: Monceau. Open: Wed to Sun 10 am to 5:30 pm. Price: €7, concessions €5. www.lesartsdecoratifs.fr

Sex Sell

Taking the 'concept store' idea to a whole new level, at sex store **1969** you can browse the beautifully laid-out merchandise and buy a bit of excitement for you and your partner, too. Choose from a wide array of sensual goods – from toys to make-up to erotic books – in the store's 100-square-metres devoted solely to sensory pleasure. Paris is the City of Love, after all, so why not make the most of your visit?

1969 Concept Store: 69 Rue Saint Martin, 75004, +33 1 42 77 69 69. Métro: Châtelet, Hôtel de Ville. Open: Mon to Fri 12 pm to 8 pm; Sat 11 am to 8 pm. www.1969.fr

Auntie Dear

Gone on a spree, now can't pay the bills? Do what the French do and go to see your 'aunt', otherwise known as the **Crédit Municipal.** This state-run pawn shop will give you somewhere around half the value of your goods so you can settle up your debts. Then, once your balance is back on the positive side, you can reclaim your things (with a small interest fee). Why the aunt moniker? 'Chez ma Tante' was what the French upper class used to say when they had to hawk their valuables for a short time to get some cash. Spread around your material wealth and get a bit of dosh, too.

Crédit Municipal: 55 Rue des Francs Bourgeois, 75004, +33 1 44 61 64 00. Métro: Rambuteau. Open: Mon to Sat 9 am to 4:30 pm. Passport and proof of residence in France for at least three months required. www.creditmunicipal.fr

Sardine Scene

Row your boat over to **La Petite Chaloupe**, whose name actually means – you guessed it – the little rowboat. It's an apt name for this shop, packed to the gills with sea-faring food products from 70 varieties of sardines to butter with algae. Choose from vintage sardines, eel fillets and monkfish liver – and even octopus sausage! If it's under the sea and it's edible, you'll likely find it here.

La Petite Chaloupe: 7 Boulevard de Port-Royal, 75013, +33 1 47 07 69 59. Métro: Les Gobelins. Open: Tues to Sat 10 am to 1:30 pm, 3 pm to 8:30 pm; Sun 10 am to 1:30 pm. 🦐

Shakespeare and Friends

No book-lover's visit to Paris is complete without going to **Shakespeare and Company**, a bookshop (and so much more) just opposite Notre Dame. Started by bibliophile George Whitman, an American who stayed in Paris after World War II and gradually amassed a large collection of English books, the shop has now grown into a platform for new writers to showcase and develop their talents. Weekly readings, film screenings, writing workshops and theatrical performances are held on a regular basis in the cosy upstairs room. Drop in to see what's on at this iconic writers' sanctuary.

Shakespeare and Company: 37 Rue de la Bûcherie, 75005, +33 1 43 25 40 93. Métro: Saint-Michel. Open: Mon to Fri 10 am to 11 pm; Sat, Sun 11 am to 11 pm. http://shakespeareandcompany.com

Pizza-Razzi

Got hollow legs? Head to **Paparazzi**, where after you cram yourself full of their two-plate pizza there won't be an inch left to spare!

It may not be exactly gourmet, but this popular restaurant is (relatively) cheap, cheerful and there's even a terrace to spread out on afterwards.

Paparazzi: 6 Square de l'Opéra Louis Jouvet, 75009, +33 1 40 07 92 56. Métro: Havre-Caumartin. Open: Mon to Sat 12 pm to 2:30 pm; Tues to Sat 7:30 pm to 10:30 pm. 🎬 👫

Picture It

With four floors showcasing contemporary photography, an auditorium, a video archive and, of course, the pre-requisite café, **The European House of Photography** is worth a visit if you're in the mood for visual stimulation. Opened in 1996, the museum hosts ever-changing temporary exhibitions in an eighteenth-century townhouse. To really delve in, take to the library and browse the collection of over 21,000 books, then head to the stone cellar for a coffee to clear your head.

Maison Européenne de la Photographie: 5-7 Rue de Fourcy, 75004, +33 1 44 78 75 00. Métro: Saint Paul or Pont Marie. Open: Wed to Sun 11 am to 8 pm. Café open Thurs to Sun 11 am to 7 pm, Wed 11 am to 5 pm. Price: €6.50, concessions €3.50. www.mep-fr.org

Dark Arts

If you're into the mystical, take a stroll over to the **Colonne Médicis** next to the Paris Stock Exchange. A 31-metre-high stone column erected in 1574 by the former queen of France Catherine de Medici, it's the only thing that remains of the Hôtel de la Reine. No-one knows exactly why the column was built or its function, but many speculate it was used by astrologer Cosimo Ruggieri, who Catherine de Medici consulted before making important decisions.

A spiral staircase leads to a platform at the top, where Ruggieri could have studied the stars. Gaze upwards and see if you can divine your own fleeting truths.

Colonne Médicis: next to Bourse de Commerce de Paris, Rue de Viarmes, 75001. Métro: Les Halles or Louvre-Rivoli.

Cool Stuff

A former refrigerated warehouse built in 1940, the concrete box of **Les Frigos** has been home to artists since the 1960s. Initially squatters, the artists were almost evicted in the 1990s despite their obvious building improvements (adding windows, building workshops and hooking up electricity). They won the right to remain, though, and today the building houses exhibitions, meetings and performances as well as many working artists. Drop in to see what's on – the door is usually open – and experience the creative process up close.

Les Frigos: 91 Rue des Frigos, 75013. Métro: Bibliothèque François Mitterrand. Open: hours vary; check website for exhibition details or email info@les-frigos.com. http://les-frigos.com ⌛

24 Hour Fact
A round-trip journey on the Seine shuttle boat service Voguéo takes 80 minutes.

14:00

Cannonball!

It's certainly not going to raise the value of your house, but having a cannonball lodged in the wall does make it something worth seeing. Now a library for decorative and fine arts, the **Hôtel de Sens** was originally constructed between 1475 and 1507 for the archbishops of Sens. Since then it's had quite a history of inhabitants, including King Henry's first wife, Queen Margot, who apparently lopped off locks of her lovers' hair to make her own wigs. But the real curiosity lies in its exterior where a nineteenth-century cannonball plunged into the front wall during the Revolution of 1830. If straining your eyes to find it has tired you out, plunk down on a bench and relax in the elaborate gardens.

Hôtel de Sens: 1 Rue du Figuier, 75004, +33 1 42 78 14 60. Métro: Pont Marie, Sully-Morland. Courtyard and library open Tues to Fri 1:30 pm to 8:30 pm; Sat 10 am to 8:30 pm. Closed Sun and Mon.

Under the Hammer

Try your luck and test your French at auction-house **Hôtel Drouot**. With almost-daily auctions, you can walk away with everything from porcelain dolls and antique books to leopard-spotted chaises. Check the website to see what's on, steel your nerves and come ready to compete – you'll be up against dealers and online bidders from around the world. A French institution since 1852, it's good fun to browse Hôtel Drouot's auction rooms even if you're not into buying.

Hôtel Drouot: Drouot Richelieu, 9 Rue Drouot, 75009, +33 1 48 00 20 20. Métro: Richelieu Drouot. Open: Mon to Sat 11 am to 6 pm. Auctions usually held Mon to Sat at 2 pm; check website for details. www.drouot.com

Sunday Tea and Artistry

Take your tea in an artist's atelier and peruse his paintings as you sip. American painter **Marcus McAllister** opens up his studio every Sunday afternoon for anyone who wants to drop by. Check out his new creations and talk to the artist himself: it's the ideal way to while away an afternoon, *n'est-ce pas?*

Sunday Tea Salon: 152 Rue Saint Maur, 75011, +33 1 49 29 08 94. Métro: Goncourt, Parmentier. Tea salon usually every Sunday 2 pm to 6 pm. Door-code is A4590, take the first stairwell on the left, up one flight of stairs, knock at the door on the right. Check website before going. www.marcusmcallister.com ⌛ 🏇

Hanging Gardens

A garden in an underground car park? Greenery exploding from a wall? It's the unexpectedness of foliage in an otherwise concrete urban jungle that grabs you when you first behold the creations of Patrick Blanc. Famed for his concept of vertical gardens – *le mur végétal* in French – this botanist developed a soil-free method of growing plants. With automated watering and fertilisation, the vegetation can thrive almost anywhere. Check out his artistry exhibited on the walls of the **Musée du Quai Branly** and hidden underground at **Parking des Ternes**.

Musée du Quai Branly: 37 Quai Branly, 75007, +33 1 56 61 70 00. Métro: Alma Marceau, Ecole Militaire. Open: Tues, Wed, Sun 11 am to 7 pm; Thurs to Sat 11 am to 9 pm. Price: €8.50; concessions €6; under 18s free. www.quaibranly.fr

Parking des Ternes: 38 Avenue des Ternes, 75017. Métro: Ternes. Open: daily, 24 hours.

Coming Up Roses

If you think only the French can master mouth-watering temptations, think again. At **Rose Bakery** – run by Brit Rose Carrarini and her French husband Jean-Charles – Parisians beat down the door for British delights like carrot cake, sticky toffee pudding and apple crumble. Located in a former storage space for market traders' carts, Rose Bakery's rustic premises and comfort food will make you feel right at home – even if home is smack in the middle of Paris.

Grab a tin of baked beans to take away from the café's small grocery store and fill your belly with the best of Britain.

Rose Bakery: 46 Rue des Martyrs, 75009, +33 1 42 82 12 80. Métro: Notre-Dame de Lorette. Open: daily (except Mon) 10 am to 4 pm.

To the Letter

See the real men behind the legends at the **Museum of Letters and Manuscripts**, where you can read the scribbles of Einstein, Debussy, John F. Kennedy and Churchill. Opened in 2004 and the first of its kind in Europe, the museum has over three floors of original documents offering rare glimpses into the creative processes and personal lives of past greats. If you fancy even more insight, you can join one of the guided tours, currently every Sunday at 3 pm.

Musée des Lettres et Manuscrits: 222 Boulevard Saint Germain, 75007, +33 1 42 22 48 48. Métro: Rue du Bac, Sèvres-Babylone, Saint-Germain-des-Prés. Open: Tues to Fri 10 am to 8 pm; Sat, Sun 10 am to 6 pm. Price: €7; concessions €5. www.museedeslettres.fr

Water, Water Everywhere

With over sixty varieties of water available, you're certainly not going to die of thirst at the **Water Bar** at Colette. While you may not be able to take their water menu seriously (the list includes a €50 bottle complete with Swarovski crystals), it's the ideal place to take a break from perusing Colette's eclectic wares. Snacks are on hand too, ranging from €7 to €17. Don't worry if you can't afford the food – there's always water!

Water Bar at Colette: 213 Rue Saint-Honoré, 75001, +33 1 55 35 33 93. Métro: Tuileries, Pyramides. Open: Mon to Sat 11 am to 7 pm. www.colette.fr

Foreign Tongue

To practise your French in a snigger-free environment, head to the drop-in conversation classes at **Cercle International de l'ARC**. ARC aims to make things easier for foreigners living in France, and what better way to do that than by helping you express yourself? Any weekday afternoon, you can join a group headed up by a French facilitator who will correct your pronunciation, assist you with your verbs and help you find *le mot juste*.

Cercle International de l'ARC: 5 Rue de l'Abbaye, 75006, +33 1 45 44 45 66. Métro: Mabillon, Saint-Germain-des-Prés. Open: Mon to Fri 2 pm to 7 pm. http://arc-cercle-international.over-blog.com

Medical Insanity

If you're in the mood for something truly extraordinary, aim straight for **Musée Fragonard**. Located within the National Veterinarian School, the museum – dedicated to anatomical oddities – is one of the oldest and strangest in France. Featuring three dancing human foetuses, a human head with coloured blood vessels and Siamese lambs, you can't help staring at the strange creatures on show.

But most horrifying of all is the collection of flayed cadavers prepared by the school's first professor of anatomy, Honoré Fragonard. Fragonard was fired by the school after they deemed him insane, but his grotesque legacy still lingers through the 21 remaining specimens.

Musée Fragonard: École Nationale Vétérinaire d'Alfort, 7 Avenue du Général de Gaulle, 94700, Maisons-Alfort, +33 1 43 96 71 72. Métro: École Vétérinaire de Maisons-Alfort. Open: Wed and Thurs 2 pm to 6 pm; Sat and Sun 1 pm to 6 pm. Price: adults €7; free for under 26s. http://musee.vet-alfort.fr

Mad for Manga

Fancy some crunch with your comics? At **Manga Café** you can eat and read at the same time. *Manga* refers to a style of comic usually produced in Japan, where the concept of cafés to relax, browse comics, grab a bite and even play video games originated.

The second biggest consumer of manga, France was keen to latch on to the café concept, too. You can entertain yourself here for hours with the largest library of manga in France, Sony Playstations, free Internet and lots of caffeinated drinks to keep you going.

Manga Café: 11 Rue des Carmes, 75005, +33 1 43 26 50 04. Métro: Maubert-Mutualité, Cluny-La Sorbonne, Saint Michel. Open: daily, Mon 2 pm to 10 pm; Tues, Wed, Fri, Sat, Sun 10:30 am to 10 pm; Thurs 2 pm to 10 pm. Price: €3 (off peak), €4 (peak) per hour. www.mangacafe.fr

Lush Lavinia

With over three floors packed with 6,000 types of wines from around the world, at **Lavinia** your brain will feel foggy before you've even started sampling! Keen to 'respect the bottle', stock is displayed flat, in a completely controlled environment – light, humidity and temperature are all set to optimal levels.

If you feel the urge to crack one open, head to the tasting bar where you can gulp any of the wines on offer. And to soak up the booze, try the restaurant's daily lunch specials.

Lavinia: 3 Boulevard de la Madeleine, 75001, +33 1 42 97 20 20. Métro: Madeleine. Open: Mon to Sat 10 am to 8 pm. Tasting bar open during store hours. Restaurant open Mon to Sat 12 pm to 3 pm. www.lavinia.fr

Dog's Dinner

You wouldn't let your pooch stroll the streets of Paris in anything less than the current trends, right? So head straight over to **Un Chien Dans le Marais**, where the latest in doggy fashion awaits. Get your loved one a tuxedo for those smart occasions, or hair-pins for that annoying fringe. Dogs may be second-class citizens in many places but in Paris they're treated like royalty. 🏃‍♀️

Un Chien Dans le Marais: 35 Bis, Rue du Roi de Sicile, 75004, +33 1 42 74 30 06. Métro: Saint-Paul. Open: daily 12 pm to 7 pm. www.unchiendanslemarais.com

Man versus Beast

Not everyone agrees with the concept, but hunting has a long and proud history. At the **Museum of Hunting and Nature**, learn all about it without getting your hands dirty or conscience sullied. Take in the 1490 painting of Phillip the Fair, renowned for his hunting abilities; browse spears from days long gone; or stare down a talking animal. You may never look at animals – or hunting – the same way again.

Musée de la Chasse et de la Nature: 62 Rue des Archives, 75003, +33 1 53 01 92 40. Métro: Hôtel de Ville, République, Rambuteau. Open: daily (except Mon) 11 am to 6 pm. Price: €6; concessions €4.50. www.chassenature.org

Dally with Dalí

Get some insight into creative genius at **Espace Dalí** in Montmartre, the largest collection of Dalí works in France. Known for his Surrealist artwork, Salvador Dalí was a resident of this area where he met Picasso, Breton and Ernst. You can see many of his drawings and sketches, as well as some of his mind-boggling sculptures. Just don't try too hard to figure out the meaning, for according to Dalí: 'There is more madness to my method than method to my madness.'

Espace Dalí: 11 Rue Poulbot, 75018, +33 1 42 64 40 10. Métro: Lamarck-Caulaincourt, Abbesses. Open: daily 10 am to 6 pm (8 pm in July and Aug). Price: adult €10; youth and students €6; under 7s free. www.daliparis.com

Play Dress Up

You treat your kids like royalty, now see what they look like dressed as one, too! At the **Jacquemart-André Museum**, they can take a turn as a marquis or a page, create and decorate their own masks, and explore nineteenth-century living all at the same time. Chock full of paintings, sculptures, tapestries and decadent furnishings, this mansion is worth a visit even if your children don't fancy life as an aristocrat.

Hit the café for more over-the-top luxury, where you can take your tea in the former grand dining room.

Musée Jacquemart-André: 158 Boulevard Haussmann, 75008, +33 1 45 62 11 59. Métro: Miromesnil, Saint-Philippe-du-Roule. Open: daily 10 am to 6 pm. Café open daily 11:45 am to 5:30 pm. Price: €11, concessions €8.50. www.musee-jacquemart-andre.com 🐾👪

Observa-Tour

Completed in 1671, the **French Observatory** is one of the oldest and largest observatories in the world. Although pollution from the City of Light means most star-gazing is now done from the observatory's two other locations (in Meudon and Nançay), the museum has been at the heart of major astronomical advancements – including the development of almanacs and modern weather maps – since its beginnings. Check out the talking clocks, follow the meridian along Cassini Hall and climb to the roof-top to see the Arago dome. *Tempus fugit* here, and the three-month queue to get in is well worth the wait.

Observatoire de Paris: 61 Avenue de l'Observatoire (entrance at 77 Avenue Denfert-Rochereau), 75014, +33 1 40 51 22 21. Métro: Denfert-Rochereau. Tours Tues, Thurs 2 pm. Reserve well in advance via visite.paris@obspm.fr. Tour telephone: +33 1 40 51 23 97. www.obspm.fr ⌛👪

Handle with Care

Get ready for some sensory action at **French Touche**, where a gallery of objects awaits your probing fingers. The creators of this concept store believe that the act of touching objects brings together creator and perceiver (or purchaser, as the case may be).

With a variety of jewellery, ceramics, cards and records by over 200 artists and designers, you'll have plenty to explore at your fingertips.

French Touche: 1 Rue Jacquemont, 75017, +33 1 42 63 31 36. Métro: La Fourche. Open: Tues to Fri 1 pm to 8 pm; Sat 11 am to 8 pm. www.frenchtouche.com

Poster Boaster

Take a piece of French film history home with you. **Gallerie Intemporel** has over 20,000 film posters for sale, as well as books and postcards from France's cinematic history. Choose a vintage poster or a reproduction, or grab a photo from the past – here, you decide who gets to be the star of your show.

La Gallerie Intemporel: 22 Rue Saint Martin, 75004, +33 1 42 72 55 41. Métro: Hôtel de Ville or Châtelet. Open: Tues to Sat 12 pm to 7 pm. www.intemporel.com

Compose Yourself

If all the art has overwhelmed you and you need a quiet place to unwind, drop into the **Public Information Library** at the Pompidou Centre. With over 400,000 documents at the ready, you can rest your feet and do a little learning, too. Read a newspaper, find a new job or listen to some music at a multi-media station. And if you're feeling creative, you can even compose your own tunes on the two available pianos.

Bibliothèque Publique d'Information (BPI): Centre Pompidou, Place Georges Pompidou, Rue Beaubourg, 75004, +33 1 44 78 12 75. Métro: Rambuteau, Hôtel de Ville, Châtelet. Open: Mon, Wed to Fri 12 pm to 10 pm; Sat, Sun 11 am to 10 pm. www.bpi.fr

On the Record

Leave the mega-stores behind and get your record-groove on at **Ground Zero**, an independent record store in Belleville. Specialising in indie and alternative – with both CDs and vinyls on offer – you can choose from soul, African, hip-hop, punk and garage. Grab a flyer for a gig and thumb the diverse collection on offer.

Ground Zero: 23 Rue Sainte Marthe, 75010, +33 1 40 03 83 08. Métro: Belleville. Open: Mon to Fri 12 pm to 8 pm; Sat 11 am to 8 pm. www.en.groundzero.fr

Chair Flair

You can't stretch out on the grass but if you're lucky enough to nab a green reclining chair then it's almost as good. Located at the **Jardin des Tuileries**, these reclining chairs are in high demand, so be prepared to stalk several recliners until its occupants leave. Then swoop in, sit down, and lean back to let the relaxing sounds of the fountain and the rays of sun wash over you.

Reclining Chairs: Jardin des Tuileries, Place de la Concorde, 75001. Métro: Tuileries or Concorde. Open: daily, April to May 7 am to 9 pm; Jun to Aug 7 am to 11 pm; Sept to March 7:30 am to 7:30 pm.

Hot Air

Rise high in the sky – 150 metres high, to be exact – with the **Air de Paris Balloon**. The hot-air balloon has been in residence in André Citroën Park since 1999, ferrying over half a million brave souls to dizzying heights. The balloon provides more than a fix for thrill seekers, though: since 2008, it has also been used to indicate air quality, turning green for good air and orange through red for poor. See Paris from above and get clued-in to what you're breathing.

Ballon Air de Paris: Parc André Citroën, 75015, +33 1 44 26 20 00. Métro: Javel or Balard. Open: daily from 9 am until 30 minutes before park closing. Park opens at 8 am daily to 5:45 pm (winter) and 9:30 pm (summer). Price: adults, €12 on holidays and weekends (all other times €10); children ages 12 to 17, €10 on holidays and weekends (all other times €9); children ages 3 to 11, €6 on holidays and weekends (all other times €5); children under 3, free. www.ballondeparis.com ⌛ 👫

Alone Time

Kids tired you out? If you need a bit of a breather – or if you want to nip off for some exploration of your own – send them on their own adventure (with a qualified local mum, of course)! **Paris Walking Tour Adventure for Kids** has a variety of options available for children to explore the Right Bank, Left Bank or 'Island Magic'.

Groups are limited to five children and guides have mobiles with them at all times. Cut the apron strings temporarily and enjoy a little downtime.

Paris Walking Tour Adventure for Kids: central Paris departure point; tour operator information and complete details available upon booking. Tours last for 3 hours and depart at 2:30 pm, returning to original point of departure. Price: from around €115 per child. For children from 7 to 12 years. www.partner.viator.com/en/7144/tours/Paris/Paris-Walking-Tour-for-Children-and-Families/d479-3151_KIDSRIGHT ⌛ 👫

Mason Magic

Recently reopened after an extensive refurbishment, the **Musée de la Franc-Maçonnerie** is the place to go if you're looking for the real story behind France's Freemasons. Created in 1889, the museum aims to educate the public on the history of Freemasonry and the contributions of its lodges to French society.

The only official Freemasons museum in France, you can learn about the origins of the group's rituals and marvel at the collection of items embroidered with the Order's symbols. Get beneath the surface of this secretive sect and pad out your Dan Brown knowledge.

Musée de la Franc-Maçonnerie: 16 Rue Cadet, 75009, +33 1 45 23 43 97. Métro: Cadet. Open: Tues to Sat 2 pm to 6 pm. Price: €6; concessions €4. www.museedelafrancmaconnerie.org

Factory Worker

Get a look into the inner workings of a tapestry factory at **Manufacture des Gobelins**, founded in the mid-1400s by Jean Gobelin and still functioning today. After Louis XIV purchased it in 1662, artisans were unified to form a royal tapestry and furniture works.

Despite a brief closure in the late 1600s and a fire which partly destroyed the building, the factory continues to spin out tapestries with the support of the French Ministry of Culture. Watch the artisans work the looms with seventeenth-century techniques as history is woven before your very eyes.

Manufacture des Gobelins: 42 Avenue des Gobelins, 75013, +33 1 44 54 19 33. Métro: Les Gobelins. Guided tours every Tues, Wed, Thurs at 2 pm and 2:45 pm. Price: €8, concessions €6. www.museums-of-paris.com/musee_en.php?code=349

24 Hour Fact
The elevators at the Eiffel Tower travel at 2 metres per second.

15:00

Classes for Lasses

Hone your bedroom moves at the **L'École des Filles de Joie**, where every Saturday afternoon you can unleash your inner stripper. Learn how to gracefully remove a glove while posing like the latest *Playboy* pin-up. Classes are open to everyone, from the painfully shy to the seasoned exhibitionist. And if you're ready for a larger audience, you can even hit the stage with the Cabaret des Filles de Joie, held every two months.

L'École des Filles de Joie: La Bellevilloise, 9-21 Rue Boyer, 75011. Métro: Gambetta, Ménilmontant. Classes every Sat 11 am to 5 pm. Price: €20. www.collectif-surprise-party.com/programme-ecole-des-filles-de-joie.html ⌛

Get Dapper

Named after Dutchman Olfert Dapper, who wrote one of the first books on Africa in the seventeenth century (despite never having left Holland!), the **Dapper Museum** is chock full of pre-colonial sculptures and artefacts from all over the Africa. Aiming to recapture Africa's rich past, the museum makes heritage come alive through interactive exhibitions such as story-telling, film and dance. Add to that a café serving fresh

African-inspired dishes and you'll feel like you're on another continent.

Musée Dapper: 35 Rue Paul Valéry, 75116, +33 1 45 00 91 75. Métro: Victor Hugo, Kléber. Open: daily (except Tues) 11 am to 7 pm. Café open 12 pm to 5 pm. Price: €6, concessions €3, under 18s free. www.dapper.com.fr

Falafel King

Although today the Marais is known for its designer boutiques and strong gay presence, it was once the centre of Paris' Jewish community. Nowhere is this more evident than on Rue des Rosiers, where small hole-in-the-wall **L'As du Fallafel** is located. Despite the encroaching trendy cafés, the street has maintained its Jewish heritage with this falafel joint at its core.

Scruffy and small, its reputation well outweighs its quarters – many believe it to be the best falafel in the world. One bite of its crunchy chickpea concoction smothered with hummous and you just might agree.

L'As du Fallafel: 34 Rue des Rosiers, 75004, +33 1 48 87 63 60. Métro: Saint-Paul. Open: daily 11 am to 7 pm (except Sat and Jewish holidays). 🌷

Down Under

Want to know what death after life is like? Head underground to the **Paris Catacombs** where you can see the bones of around 5 million skeletons who were laid here to rest. As Paris grew and space shrank, a network of quarries and tunnels under the city was deemed the answer to Paris' burial problem. Opened in the late 1700s, this underground ossuary was quickly populated by those killed in riots and relocated residents of Paris' cemeteries. Although the last bones to call this home were buried in 1814, the catacombs have been in continuous use as concert halls, French Resistance hideaways and German bunkers during World War II. Wander through the maze-like tunnels packed with skulls and stare death in the face.

Paris Catacombs: 1 Avenue du Colonel Henri Rol-Tanguy, Place Denfert Rochereau, 75014, +33 1 43 22 47 63. Métro: Denfert-Rochereau. Open: Tues to Sun 10 am to 5 pm. Price: adult €8, ages 14 to 26 €4, under 13s free. www.carnavalet.paris.fr 🚻

Berri Good

Well known for French films *Jean de Florette* and *Manon of the Spring*, director Claude Berri was also passionate about contemporary art. At his gallery **Espace Claude Berri**, you can see artworks from his personal collection (some of which include Picasso, Dalí and Giacometti) as well as an ever-changing programme featuring new contemporary artists. Drop by and see how this cinematic great helped breathe new life into the Paris' art scene.

Espace Claude Berri: 8 Rue Rambuteau, 75003, +33 1 44 54 88 50. Métro: Rambuteau. Open: Tues to Sat 11 am to 7 pm. Closed August. Price: free. www.espace-claudeberri.com ⧗

After-Life Confessions

As large in death as in life, artist and diarist Marie Bashkirtseff's grave in the **Passy Cemetery** has been declared a historic monument. A true-to-life artist's studio stands atop her plot, reflecting her love for painting. Although Bashkirtseff produced several well-known paintings, she is more famous for her tell-all diary detailing the difficulties of women artists in mid-nineteenth century aristocratic society. Dying at age 26, she was an influential figure among the Parisian intellectuals, writing under a *nom de plume* for feminist papers.

Her diary *I am the Most Interesting Book of All* can still be purchased today, and the original version is held at the National Library.

Marie Bashkirtseff: Cimetière de Passy, 2 Rue du Commandant Schlœsing, 75116. Métro: Trocadéro. Open: Mon to Fri 8 am to 6 pm, Sat 8:30 am to 6 pm, Sun 9 am to 6 pm (until 5:30 pm in winter). Price: free.

Send in the Clowns

Had enough of trying to figure out modern art at nearby Pompidou Centre? Cross the pedestrian square to **Café Beaubourg**, another restaurant founded by the infamous Costes brothers.

Sit outside on the terrace where you can indulge in some old-fashioned fun by watching mimes and jugglers, along with the oh-so-cool neighbouring diners. And if you're ready

for more minimalism, head inside where the lofty ceilings
and cement floors echo the museum next door.

Café Beaubourg: 100 Rue St-Martin, 75004, +33 1 48 87 63 96. Métro:
Rambuteau or Hôtel de Ville. Open: Mon to Fri 8 am to 1 am; Sat, Sun
8 am to 2 am. 🦐

Veggie Heaven

If you're craving something besides the usual slim pickings
of vegetarian options most French restaurants have on offer,
go to **Le Potager du Marais**. Its lengthy menu of organic
food ranges from traditional French cuisine vegetarian-style
to more exotic fare. Slide into the communal table, have a
wheat-grass shake, and let your tastebuds delight as the
veggies take centre stage.

Le Potager du Marais: 22 Rue Rambuteau, 75003, +33 1 42 74 24 66. Métro:
Rambuteau. Open: daily 12 pm to 12 am. 🦐

In the Mood

Get a little bit of loving at the **Museum of Romantic Life**,
where the surroundings are every bit as romantic as what's
on display. Housed in the former mansion of painter Ary
Scheffer, the museum traces the history of the Romantic
Movement, focusing in particular on novelist George Sand.
Set away from the hustle and bustle of nearby Pigalle with
a garden full of lilacs and roses, even the most hardened of
hearts can't help but feel a twinge of emotion.

Musée de la Vie Romantique: Hôtel Scheffer-Renan, 16 Rue Chaptal, 75009, +33 1 55 31 95 67. Métro: Saint-Georges, Pigalle, Blanche. Open: daily (except Mon) 10 am to 6 pm. Price: free. www.vie-romantique.paris.fr

Worlds Away

Hit the books at the **French National Library**. A repository for pretty much everything ever published in France, the library has been at its current home since 1995 and holds more than 20 million volumes. Head to the reading rooms to browse materials like ancient Greek documents or the bilingual collection *France in America,* outlining France's presence in the New World across the centuries.

If you tire of books, take in the stunning collection of Coronelli globes on display in the west entrance hall, presented to Louis XIV in 1683.

Bibliothèque Nationale de France, François-Mitterrand: Quai François-Mauriac, 75706, + 33 1 53 79 59 59. Métro: Quai de la Gare. Open: Mon 2 pm to 7 pm; Tues to Sat 9 am to 7 pm; Sun 1 pm to 7 pm. One day card for entry to reading rooms: €3.30. Ages 18 and over; identification must be provided. See website for details. Globes exhibition open Tues to Sat 10 am to 7 pm; Sun 1 pm to 7 pm. www.bnf.fr

Flour Power

Everyone's heard of the infamous Moulin Rouge, but in its day the **Moulin de la Galette** was the true belle of the ball, posing for painters like Renoir (*Bal du Moulin de la Galette)* and Van Gogh (*Le Moulin de la Galette)*. Used to grind flour, the mill relied on two windmills for power: the *Radet* and

Blute-fin. Over the years, the building has been used as a dance hall and a television studio before being sold into private hands. The spirit of the Moulin lives on, though, at the new Moulin de la Galette, now a restaurant and topped with the original *Radet* windmill, moved from its original location in 1924.

Moulin du Radet: Le Moulin de la Galette, 83 Rue Lepic, 75018, +33 1 46 06 84 77. Métro: Abbesses, Lamarck-Caulaincourt. Open: daily 12 pm to 11 pm. www.lemoulindelagalette.eu 🍸

In Studio

Soak up some cinematic history at **Studio 28**, Paris' first arthouse cinema. Opened in 1928, artists such as Jean Cocteau (who designed the lamp fixtures) and Luis Buñuel (whose film *L'Âge d'Or* practically caused riots the first time it was shown) have all crossed its threshold.

The cinema has been modernised with the usual luxuries but don't expect to find any popcorn here – instead, choose from the selection of tarts and cakes and relax in the heated garden with the ghosts of past cinematic greats.

Studio 28: 10 Rue Tholozé, 75018, +33 1 46 06 36 07. Métro: Blanche, Abbesses. Matinées usually at 3 pm; check website for details. Price: €8, concessions €6.80. www.cinemastudio28.com ⧗

Under the Sea

Dance like a jellyfish, act ferocious like a shark or paint an ocean scene on a wall – at the **Cinéacqua**, there's 500 species of fish to look at and oh-so-much more to keep the young ones entertained. Go google-eyed at the 25 sharks in a tank filled with 3 million litres of water, catch a film at the Movieum, or eat a meal beside a fish tank. Here, you can get close to the creatures of the sea – and even reach out and touch them, if you're brave enough.

Cinéacqua: 5 Avenue Albert de Mun, 75016, +33 1 40 69 23 23. Métro: Trocadéro. Open: Oct to Mar, daily 10 am to 6 pm; Apr to Sep, daily 10 am to 7 pm. Price: €19.50; concessions €12.50 to €15.50; free for under 3s. www.cineaqua.com 🏃

Get Steamy

Scrub off the day's dirt and get a new glow at the **O'Kari** steam baths. Just for women, this modern hammam is located in the cellar of an eighteenth century building. While that might sound a bit claustrophobic, founder Karima Lasfar has combined Algerian aesthetics with contemporary design, resulting in a space that's inviting and surprisingly spacious. Hit the steam rooms to get rid of your toxins, then slough off dead skin. Smooth yourself with olive oil from Northern Algeria and treat your hair to a mask.

By the end of your three hours here, you'll emerge from the underground rooms a new person.

O'Kari: 22 Rue Dessoubs, 75002, +33 1 42 36 94 66. Métro: Réaumur-Sébastopol. Open: daily 10 am to 8 pm. By appointment only. http://o-kari.com ⧗

Putting on the Retz

Fashion designers, architects, painters and scientists all come together at the unique exhibition space that is the **Passage de Retz**. Located within the seventeenth century Hôtel de Retz, this gallery is dedicated to contemporary art in all its forms. Grab a drink at the café then make your way through the interlinking rooms where the space itself is as much a work of art as what's on display. From the soaring glass ceiling of the Orangery to the lush green of the garden, you won't want to leave one of Paris' most hidden – and idyllic – art galleries.

Passage de Retz: 9 Rue Charlot, 75003, +33 1 48 04 37 99. Métro: Filles du Calvaire. Open: Tues to Sat 10 am to 7 pm. Price: €8. www.passagederetz.com 🎺

Shakespeare à la France

No matter where you are, you can't escape the Bard of the English language – even in France! Every summer, the **Shakespeare Garden** in the Bois de Bologne is the fitting location for open-air performances of Shakespeare (in both English and French). The garden is composed of five smaller plots, each named after Shakespeare's plays and each containing relevant plants: a moor-like space with heather in the *Macbeth* garden; Danish plants in the *Hamlet* garden. See one of the greatest English writers of all time performed in a strikingly authentic yet foreign location.

Jardin Shakespeare: Chapiteau Alexis Gruss, Allée de la Reine Marguerite, Bois de Boulogne, 75016, +33 1 40 19 95 33. Métro: Porte Maillot. Performance times vary; plays usually start at 12:30 pm, 3 pm or 5:30 pm. Check website for details. Season usually runs from May to October. www.jardinshakespeare.fr ⌛

Hit the Ice

Chill out and get some exercise at **Patinoire de Boulogne**, an ice-skating rink that's open all year round. Go with the kids for an afternoon session or head there at night for the ice-disco and infamous 'foam party'.

And if you want to play rough, you can try out some hockey on Saturday mornings.

Patinoire Boulogne-Billancourt: 1 Rue Victor-Griffuelhes, 92100, Boulogne-Billancourt, +33 1 46 08 00 88. Métro: Marcel Sembat, Billancourt. Open: hours vary; check website for details. Family skates held mostly on weekends 3 pm to 6 pm; foam party Wed at 9 pm; ice disco Sat at 9 pm. Hockey every Sat morn at 7:45 am for beginners; 9 am for others. Price: €5.50; concessions €4.60. Skate hire available on site. www.patinoireboulogne.com ⌛👪

Asia Fantasia

Get your Oriental art fix at **Musée Guimet**. Founded in 1879 by industrialist and Far East enthusiast Émile Étienne Guimet, the museum has one of the largest collections of Asian art outside of Asia. Sate your senses with over 1600 Himalayan pieces and 20,000 Chinese artworks spanning seven millennia. If you feel the need for fresh air but you don't want to leave the Far East behind, head over to the nearby Japanese Garden for a tranquil cuppa in the Tea Pavilion.

Musée Guimet: 6 Place d'Iéna, 75016, +33 1 56 52 53 00. Métro: Iéna or Boissière. Open: daily (except Tues) 10 am to 6 pm. Price: €7.50, €5.50 concessions, free for under 18s. www.guimet.fr

Tea Pavilion: The Buddist Panthéon, 19 Avenue d'Iéna, 75116, +33 1 40 73 88 00. Open daily (except Tues) from 9:45 am to 5:45 pm. Price: free.

Burnt Offerings

Displayed like jewellery behind a shiny glass case, the pastries and bon-bons at **Pierre Hermé** look almost too good to eat. If you can't bring yourself to destroy perfection one bite at a time, don't worry – now, you can purchase a sweet-smelling candle to enjoy the sugary odours at home. Choose from Sucre de Bois, created with perfumer Olivia Giacobetti with a sugar, maple and vanilla; or Herbe d'amandes with a tonka bean and yerba maté scent. Just don't burn the candles when hungry: remember, wax is not easily digestible!

Pierre Hermé: 72 Rue Bonaparte, 75006, +33 1 43 54 47 77. Métro: Saint-Sulpice. Open: daily 10 am to 7 pm (Sat until 7:30 pm). Candles from €26. www.pierreherme.com

16:00

Way Up High

You can't miss department store **Galeries Lafayette** at its place of pride on Boulevard Haussmann. But you can miss its hidden roof terrace, where you can gaze down on the city – at the same height as the first level of the Eiffel Tower – without the bother of having to queue. Take the lift to the highest floor then climb a flight of stairs and you're on top of the world. Spot the memorial to Jules Védrines, the first man to land a plane on a city building at this very spot, then grab a chair and take in the view. With snacks and drinks at the ready and ten storeys of luxury goods beneath you, what could be better?

Galeries Lafayette: 40 Boulevard Haussmann, 75009, +33 1 42 82 34 56. Métro: Chaussée d'Antin-Lafayette. Open: Mon to Sat 9:30 am to 8 pm (Thurs till 9 pm). www.galerieslafayette.com 🏊 👫

Tree Treasure

It's got a great view of Notre Dame and it's a perfect place to get some shade in the summer, but **Square René Viviani-**

Montebello is worth a visit for more than that: the oldest tree in Paris took root around 400 years ago in its south-west corner. Now supported by concrete pillars, the *Robinia Pseudoacacia* (otherwise known as the black locust tree) was apparently planted in 1601 by Jean Robin, who introduced the tree to France. Despite losing branches during World War I shelling, the tree still blooms every year.

Oldest tree in Paris: Square René Viviani-Montebello, 2 Rue du Fouarre, 75005. Métro: Cluny-La Sorbonne. Open: Mon to Fri 8 am to 5 pm, Sat and Sun 9 am to 5 pm (winter); Mon to Fri 8 am to 8:30 pm, Sat and Sun 9 am to 8:30 pm (summer).

Pomp it Up

With eye-popping coloured tubes wrapped around a glass building, the outside of the **Pompidou Centre** is as much a work of contemporary art as its contents.

Two young architects – Italian Renzo Piano and Brit Richard Rogers – won a competition to build this new space entirely devoted to contemporary art. Their design was trumpeted by *The New York Times* as having 'turned the architecture world upside down.'

The centre opened in 1977 as the brainchild of President Georges Pompidou. To date, over 150 million visitors have flocked to see artwork by modern greats from Matisse to Man Ray. Hit the roof for Restaurant Georges where, in keeping with the theme, the restaurant inside – decorated with undulating aluminium sheeting – is as interesting as the panoramic views outside.

Centre Pompidou: 75004, +33 1 44 78 12 33. Métro: Rambuteau, Hôtel de Ville, Châtelet. Open: daily (except Tues) 11 am to 9 pm. Price €10 or €12 (depending on season), €9 or €8 concessions. To book the restaurant: +33 1 44 78 47 99. www.centrepompidou.fr

Lose Your Locks

If your budget just can't accommodate expensive haircuts, head to the **Toni & Guy Academy** where you can get your locks lopped for free if you book in as a model. Most stylists already have some experience, so all you'll have to worry about is your French. And if it all does go wrong, never fear – there are plenty of cafés nearby to help you drown your sorrows.

Toni & Guy Academy: 18 Rue Tiquetonne, 75002, +33 1 40 41 11 00. Métro: Étienne Marcel. Call to book an appointment.

Towering Fear

Jean Sans Peur (Jean 'Without Fear') was so afraid of revenge attacks after he killed his cousin – the brother of King Charles VI – he built a tower to protect himself.

It didn't work very well, though: after 30 years of civil war triggered by the murder, Jean was assassinated in 1419. Climb the tower's spiral staircase and examine Jean's defensive manoeuvres for yourself, learning about life in France and medieval architecture on the way.

Tour Jean Sans Peur: 20 Rue Etienne-Marcel, 75002, +33 1 40 26 20 28. Métro: Étienne Marcel. Open: Nov to Mar: Wed, Sat, Sun 1:30 pm to 6 pm; Apr to Oct: Wed to Sun 1:30 pm to 6 pm. Price: €5; concessions €3; free for under 7s. Tour €8. www.tourjeansanspeur.com 👬

Cupcake Crazy

With all the beautiful pastries on offer in Paris, it might seem slightly sacrilegious to crave a cupcake. But at **Cupcakes & Co**, you can have your little bite of cake and experience Paris, too: these are cupcakes with a French twist. With all organic ingredients and flavours such as jasmine-orange and chocolate passion-fruit, Rebecca and Maggie Bellity's shop is the first of its kind in pastry-ridden Paris. Check out the cute pink facade and sample some of the goodies within without letting down your gourmet taste-buds.

Cupcakes & Co: 25 Rue de la Forge Royale, 75011, +33 1 43 67 16 19. Métro: Faidherbe-Chaligny. Open: Tues to Sat 10 am to 7 pm. http://cupcakesandco.fr 🍴 👬

Mark the Spot

Considered by some to be the finest example of Neoclassical architecture in Paris, **Chapelle Expiatoire** stands on the first burial site of Queen Marie Antoinette and King Louis XVI. After the couple's deaths at the guillotine in 1793, their remains were dumped in a pit at the then-cemetery. The land was later purchased by a magistrate and the bodies were eventually dug up and moved to a more fitting location – the Basilique Saint-Denis – but the chapel was constructed in their honour. Finished in 1826, it contains gleaming white marble statues of the King and Queen, and the black-and-white marble altar is said to indicate their exact burial spot.

Even though they've moved on, others remain: the bodies of 3,000 other victims of the Revolution are buried in the chapel grounds, their graves sheltered by different species of trees each representing the classes of those who died.

Chapelle Expiatoire: 29 Rue Pasquier, 75008, +33 1 44 32 18 00. Métro: Saint-Augustin. Open: Thurs to Sat 1 pm to 5 pm. Price: €5; concessions €3.50; free for under 18s. http://chapelle-expiatoire.monuments-nationaux.fr ⌛

All in the Family

For a spot of peace and some ice cream to boot, cross the footbridge to Île Saint-Louis and head over to **Berthillon**. You may have to queue, but once you get your tongue around the creamy rich flavours (chocolate mandarin and pear caramel, for a start) produced by the three generations of *glaciers*, it'll all be worth it. Grab your cone and find a quiet corner to indulge in sheer ice-cream heaven.

Berthillon: 29-31 Rue Saint Louis en l'Île, 75004, +33 1 43 54 31 61. Métro: Pont Marie. Open: Wed to Sun 10 am to 8 pm. www.berthillon.fr 🍧 👫

Shed Some Light

The Arab World Institute has been promoting understanding and awareness between France and 22 Arab nations since 1980. Perched by the Seine, the large rectangular structure is covered with geometric designs that are actually small windows acting like camera lenses, opening and closing every hour to allow light into the building. Head straight to the museum to learn about the Arab world from pre-Islamic times to the present, taking in ancient costumes and astronomical equipment as you go. If the filtered light makes you drowsy, hit the roof to catch some rays, see great views over Notre Dame and sip some mint tea.

Institut du Monde Arabe: 1 Rue des Fossés-Saint-Bernard, Place Mohammed-V, 75005, +33 1 40 51 38 38. Métro: Jussieu, Cardinal Lemoine. Open: daily (except Mon) 10 am to 6 pm. Library open daily (except Sun, Mon) 1 pm to 8 pm. Panoramic Restaurant (9th floor) open 11 am to 11:30 pm, +33 1 55 42 55 42. www.imarabe.org

24 Hour Fact

It would take around 24 days, using every hour in the day, to briefly view all the exhibits in the Louvre.

Belle View

Flee the packed tourist sites and get some quiet at **Belleville Park**. At 108 metres, it's the highest park in Paris and it has the stunning panoramic views across the city to prove it. See the longest waterfall fountain in Paris, learn about the importance of clean air at the **Maison de l'Air**, or hit some balls around on the ping-pong tables. As you wander between the packed flower beds – prepared for their flowers two years ahead of time – you'll feel like you've found a little piece of Parisian heaven.

Parc de Belleville: 75020. Métro: Couronnes, Belleville, Pyrénées. Open: Mon to Fri from 8 am; Sat, Sun from 9 am to around dusk.

Maison de l'Air: 27 Rue Piat, 75020, +33 1 43 28 47 63. Métro: Couronnes. Open: Oct to Mar, Tues to Sun 1:30 pm to 5 pm; from April to Sept, 1:30 pm to 5:30 pm (until 6:30 pm weekends). Price: free. ⏳ 👫

The Green Fairy

If you're a fan of absinthe – the notorious spirit beloved by many Parisian bohemian artists – then **Vert d'Absinthe** is the shop for you. Dedicated to all things absinthe, you can browse the collection of old bottles, fancy glasses and advertisements from days gone by.

And if you want to imbibe, don't worry: although the liquid was thought to contain dangerous psychoactive drugs, it's now been proven as safe as any other spirit. Have a swig and let the green fairy carry you away.

Vert d'Absinthe: 11 Rue d'Ormesson, 75004, +33 1 42 71 69 73. Métro: Saint-Paul. Open: Tues to Sat 12 pm to 7 pm. www.vertdabsinthe.com

Hugo's House

Famous for his novels *The Hunchback of Notre Dame* and *Les Miserables*, Victor Hugo was one of the most influential French men of his time. The popularity of his writing, in particular *The Hunchback of Notre Dame*, drew so many tourists to the neglected cathedral that authorities were obliged to restore it! He and his wife rented an apartment at **Hôtel de Rohan-Guéménée** in the Place des Vosges from 1832 to 1848, and it is here you can see how the literary legend lived. Hugo wrote part of *Les Mis* in these rooms and as you wander through the furnished apartment – walls lined with drawings, photos and other memorabilia of his life – you can almost imagine the great writer still working away.

Maison de Victor Hugo: Hôtel de Rohan-Guéménée, 6 Place des Vosges, 75004, +33 1 42 72 10 16. Métro: Saint-Paul. Open: Tues to Sun 10 am to 6 pm. Price: free. www.musee-hugo.paris.fr

Sell Your Stuff

Get rid of the old and make way for the new without the fuss of doing it yourself: eBay consignment shop **EncherExpert** will sell your unwanted items for you. Cart your things over to one of their nine stores city-wide or, if it's too big to carry, they'll come get it for free. You owe them nothing until they sell your item; then, they take 33% of the price your item achieves, plus a €5 listing fee.

Your cheque comes three to four weeks later – along with a *carte blanche* to hit the shops again!

EncherExpert: 43 Boulevard Saint Marcel, 75013, +33 1 55 43 80 16. Métro: Saint-Marcel. Open: Tues to Sat 11 am to 1:30 pm; 3 pm to 7 pm. Other locations city-wide; check website for details. www.encherexpert.com

Hats On

Try a ready-made hat on for size or get one made to measure at French millinery expert **Estelle Ramousse**. From 1930s creations to more fashion-forward felts complete with feathers, there's a hat here for every head. With years of training in theatrical costume design, a chapeau by Ramousse gives any outfit the necessary touch of drama.

Estelle Ramousse: 64 Rue de la Mare, 75020, +33 1 77 11 29 04. Métro: Pyrénées. Open: by appointment. www.chapeausurmesure.com

Get Creative

Make like Monet and get out your canvas and brushes to capture some of Paris' charm. Don't worry if you've left them at home – at **Sennelier,** you can stock up on brushes, oil paints and watercolours to your artistic heart's content.

Gustave Sennelier, who opened the shop in 1887, was fascinated by the chemistry of colours. In collaboration with painters – including Cezanne – Sennelier developed 100 shades of colour, ground by hand in an intensive process. In 1949 the shop even designed a product just for Picasso: an oil pastel that wouldn't smudge. Today, the shop is still run by the Sennelier family and although the production of paints has been modernised, the history of its famous past customers still lingers in the air.

Sennelier: 3 Quai Voltaire, 75007, +33 1 42 60 72 15. Métro: St-Germain-des-Prés. Open: Mon 2 pm to 6:30 pm; Tues to Sat 10 am to 12:45 pm, 2 pm to 6:30 pm. www.magasinsennelier.fr.

Green Machine

Forget about your carbon-footprint: now, you can tour Paris guilt-free in a clean, green machine. **EcoVisit's Paris by Day** will show you the sights with a chauffeured tour in a hybrid Prius. Take in the first office building in the world with LED lights, learn about the return of the fish to the Seine, and see all the big tourist attractions, too. Buckle up and zip about town with a clear conscience.

EcoVisit's Paris by Day: +33 1 77 13 79 99. Meet at Place de la Concorde, in front of Tuileries entrance. Métro: Concorde. Departures at 9 am, 10 am, 11 am, 3 pm, 4 pm and 5 pm all year long except 14th July. Tour lasts for one hour and must be booked at least 48 hours in advance. Price: €80 per car. www.ecovisitparis.com ⌛

Hop On

Duck into the Place du Palais Royal for a little fun and games with **Buren's Columns** (also known as Les Deux Plateaux). Designed in the mid-eighties by artist Daniel Buren, the black and white marble columns of varying sizes provoked controversy amongst French right-wingers who felt the contemporary installation rejected France's rich architectural past. The columns are still a touchy subject today: Buren has insisted they be removed due to neglect and lack of maintenance. They're there for now, though, so take a leap from one to the other while you can. Legend has it if you throw a coin onto the highest column, your wish will come true.

Colonnes de Buren: Place du Palais Royal, 75001. Métro: Palais Royal-Musée du Louvre. Open: June 1 to Aug 31, 7 am to 11 pm; Sept, 7 am to 9:30 pm; Oct 1 to May 31, 7:30 am to 8:30 pm.

24 Hour Fact
Basic hours of business in Paris are 8 or 9 am to 6:30 or 7:30 pm.

17:00

Architectural Giant

If staring at all the old buildings around Paris still hasn't fulfilled your architectural cravings, head to the **City of Architecture** at the Palais de Chaillot. Here you can see life-sized plaster casts of existing civil and religious buildings constructed in various styles, from Roman to Renaissance; examine murals and stained glass in recreated chapels and crypts; and enter a to-scale replica of an apartment from Le Corbusier's famous Cité Radieuse in Marseille. The largest museum dedicated to architecture in the world, it's guaranteed to impress even the most blasé builder.

Cité de l'Architecture et du Patrimoine: Palais de Chaillot, 1 Place du Trocadéro, 75116, +33 1 58 51 52 00. Métro: Trocadéro. Open: Mon, Wed, Fri to Sun 11 am to 7 pm; Thurs 11 am to 9 pm. Price: €8; concessions €5; free for under 18s. www.citechaillot.fr

Be Square

It's the oldest square in Paris and the ideal place to catch your breath before gearing up for the night ahead. Built by Henri IV from 1605 to 1612, **Place des Vosges** – with the perfect dimensions of 140 metres by 140 metres – has been the square of choice for many of France's famous artists (including Mme de Sévigné, Victor Hugo and Georges Dufrénoy), who resided in the uniform red-bricked buildings that surround it.

Plop on a bench under the shade of a linden tree, listen to the sound of the fountains and let the dusk descend.

Place des Vosges: 75003. Métro: Bastille, Chemin Vert, Saint-Paul. Open: daily until dusk.

Gallery in the Galerie

For serious consumers, shopping is an art in itself. Galeries Lafayette takes it one step further with **La Galerie des Galeries**, an art gallery hidden away behind women's wear on the first floor. Take a break from the heady pursuit of the perfect ensemble and check out works by contemporary designers of art, fashion and design in this gleaming white space. Here, money is literally no object.

La Galerie des Galeries: first floor Galeries Lafayette, 40 Boulevard Haussmann, +33 1 42 82 81 98. Métro: Chaussée d'Antin-Lafayette. Open: Mon to Sat 9:30 am to 8 pm (Thurs to 9 pm). Price: free. www.galerieslafayette.com

Film Fantastic

Want to go where the sun don't shine? Head into the vast underground complex of the Forum des Halles and make your way to the **Forum des Images** where for €5 you can fill your eyes with everything to do with film – and Paris. The Forum des Images holds a vast collection of every image produced since 1895 with any connection to Paris, culminating in over 4,000 hours of footage. Check out the website to see what's on or drop by and try your luck – with five theatres as well as a François Truffaut library on-site, there's sure to be something to entertain.

Forum des Images: Forum des Halles, 2 Rue du Cinema, 75001, +33 1 44 76 63 00. Métro: Les Halles. Open: Tues to Fri 12:30 pm to 11:30 pm; Sat, Sun 2 pm to 11:30 pm. Bar open weekdays 12:30 pm to 9 pm; weekend 2:15 pm to 9 pm. Collection rooms open Tues to Fri 12:30 pm to 10 pm; weekend 2 pm to 10 pm. Price: €5, €4 for under 12s. www.forumdesimages.net

Play Pétanque

Throw some balls around and have a drink at canal-side **Bar Ourcq**. The game of pétanque, where players stand with their feet together and lob metal spheres towards a small wooden ball, is played by around 17 million people in France.

If your hand-eye coordination diminishes glass by glass, then take a break and listen to the sounds of the DJs who come on at night.

Bar Ourcq: 68 Quai de la Loire, 75019, +33 1 42 40 12 26. Métro: Laumière. Open: Wed, Thurs 3 pm to 12 am; Fri, Sat 3 pm to 2 am; Sun 3 pm to 10 pm. http://barourcq.free.fr

Tea History

Famed for their invention of the 'double decker' macaron – two cookie-like discs filled with *ganache* – tea-time at **Ladurée**'s original Rue Royale tearoom is every bit as scrumptious as their pastry creations. One of the first tearooms to open in Paris in 1862, it grew quickly in popularity as a place for women to gather (cafés were dominated by men). Using techniques from the Sistine Chapel and the newly built Garnier opera house, the ceiling was covered with frescoes you can still see as you sip.

Drink in the old-world elegance as your taste-buds delight.

Ladurée: 16 Rue Royale, 75008, +33 1 42 60 21 79. Métro: Concorde. Open: Mon to Thurs 8:30 am to 7:30 pm; Fri, Sat 8:30 am to 8 pm; Sun 10 am to 7 pm. Price: tea from around €6.50; macarons from around €2. www.laduree.com 🐾

Twin Cinemas

If one cinema just isn't enough, head down to the **Bassin de la Villette** where you get two in one go. The largest artificial lake in Paris, the Bassin de la Villette was created in 1808 as a back-up for Paris' drinking water supply. Now, it's home to the MK2 cinemas (the Quai de Seine and the Quai de Loire) which straddle each side of the rectangular reservoir.

Showing a wide variety of arthouse films – with three restaurants, 12 screens and a bookstore between them –

you'll be hard pressed to choose one over the other. Don't worry if you can't decide: electric ferry *Zéro de Conduite* (free for ticket-holders) zips film-goers back and forth. Snuggle into the 'love-seats' (two-seaters) at the Quai de Loire then take a moon-lit ride across the water for a bite at the Quai de Seine. Here, it's double the cinematic fun.

MK2 Quai de Seine cinema: 14 Quai de la Seine, 75019, +33 8 92 69 84 84. Métro: Stalingrad, Jaurès. Check website for programme; most films start around 5:30 pm, 8 pm and 10 pm. Price: adults €10.50, under 18s €5.90, under 10s €5. www.mk2.com ⏳

MK2 Quai de Loire: 7 Quai de la Loire,75019, +33 8 92 69 84 84. Métro: Stalingrad, Jaurès. Check website for programme. Price: adults €10.50, under 18s €5.90, under 10s €5. www.mk2.com ⏳

Something Old, Something New

One look into concept store **Le 66** and although you may be blinded by the gleaming steel, you'll know it's not just another traditional upscale Champs-Elysée shop. Spread out over four floors with a mix of old and new items – including books, music and clothing labels from Alexander McQueen to Acne – it's *the* place for fashion-forward Parisians.

The store's even open Sundays if you just can't get enough.

Le 66: 66 Avenue des Champs-Elysées, 75008, +33 1 53 53 33 80. Métro: George V. Open: Mon to Fri 11 am to 8 pm, Sat 11:30 am to 8:30 pm, Sun 2 pm to 8 pm. www.le66.fr

Swedish Escape

Fed up with French cuisine? Try a taste of Sweden at the **Swedish Café**, located inside the Swedish Institute at the heart of the Marais. Grab a seat in the white minimalistic interior or a table in the courtyard outside. Munch a piece of carrot cake and test one of the traditional Swedish recipes. And if you're hungry for more, head inside to feast your eyes on 600 paintings by Swedish greats Gustaf Lundberg and Alexander Roslin.

Le Café Suédois: Hôtel de Marle, 11 Rue Payenne, 75003, +33 1 44 78 80 11. Métro: Saint-Paul, Chemin Vert. Open: Tues to Sun 12 pm to 6 pm. www.si.se 🎭

Swedish Institute: 11 Rue Payenne, 75003, + 33 1 44 78 80 20. Métro: Saint-Paul, Chemin Vert. Open: daily (except Mon) 12 pm to 6 pm.

A Little Bit of Corsetry

If you're looking for the real thing when it comes to lingerie, look no further: at **Alice Cadolle**, five generations of expert corset-makers have produced extraordinary garments that look so good you won't want to cover them up! Founded in 1889 by Herminie Cadolle – who is said to have actually invented the bra – the ready-to-wear shop on Rue Cambon offers luxurious bras and corsets. To make even more of a lasting impression, head over to the couture shop on Rue Saint-Honoré where you can fashion your own bedtime creation with their made-to-measure service.

Alice Cadolle: 4 Rue Cambon, 75001, +33 1 42 60 94 22. Métro: Concorde or Madeleine. Open: Mon to Sat 10 am to 6:30 pm. Couture shop at 255 Rue St-Honoré, 75001, +33 1 42 60 94 94. Métro: Concorde. Open: Mon to Fri 10 am to 1 pm, 2 pm to 6:30 pm (by appointment). www.cadolle.fr. ⌛

Oldie with Goodies

Trading since the early 1600s, **Le Marché des Enfants Rouge** is one of the oldest street markets in Paris. Named after the red uniforms of children in a nearby orphanage, this small but perfectly formed covered market is chock-full of temptations, from freshly made Moroccan takeaways to aromatic flowers. Wander between the stalls and try not to let your stomach take control of the purse-strings!

Le Marché des Enfants Rouges: 39 Rue de Bretagne (enter on Rue Charlot), 75003. Métro: Filles du Calvaire, Temple. Open: Tues to Sat 8:30 am to 1 pm, 4 pm to 7:30 pm (until 8 pm Fri and Sat), Sun 8:30 to 2 pm.

Arts and Crafts

See how everyday items can be things of beauty at the **Museum of Decorative Arts**. With over 150,000 objects – including everything from tie-pins to doll houses – your eyes will struggle to take in the parade of goods on display from the Middle Ages to the present. Head to the 'period rooms', where you can see part of French designer Jeanne Lanvin's house or the bedroom of a nineteen-century courtesan. And if your senses still aren't sated, check out the Publicity & Fashion and Textile wings within the same building.

Musée des Arts Décoratif: 107 Rue de Rivoli, 75001, +33 1 44 55 57 50.
Métro: Palais Royal-Musée du Louvre, Tuileries, Pyramides. Open: Tues to
Sun 11 am to 6 pm (until 9 pm on Thurs). Price: €9, concessions €7.50.
www.lesartsdecoratifs.fr

Kitchen Fairy

If you're seeking something quirky for your kitchen, you're
bound to come across it at **Au Petit Bonheur de la Chance**.
Stuffed to the gills with all things kitchen-related from vintage
cups to old-school salt pots, the kitchen fairy within will go
nuts at all the treasures on display. Grab some jam jars or a
stripy café-au-lait mug and head for home.

Au Petit Bonheur de la Chance: 13 Rue Saint-Paul, 75004, +33 1 42 74 36
38. Métro: Saint-Paul. Open: daily (except Tues and Wed) 11 am to 1 pm,
2:30 pm to 7 pm.

Hand-me-Down Luxury

Want a little bit of luxury without the price tag? Buy some
Chanel or Hermès without breaking the bank at second-
hand luxury-goods shop **Dépot Vente**. With a wide variety
of women's and men's goods available, you can choose
anything from designer ties or handbags to raincoats and
pumps. After all, when it's Louis Vuitton or Dior, does it really
matter if it's been worn before?

Dépot Vente du 17e: 109 Rue de Courcelles, 75017, +33 1 40 53 80 82.
Métro: Courcelles. Open: Tues to Sat 10:30 am to 7:30 pm; Mon 2 pm to
7:30 pm. www.depot-vente-paris.fr

Buzz Around

If you want to get serious about sight-seeing, take to the sky with **HéliParis**'s 30-minute tour of Paris and beyond. Look down on the Eiffel Tower and get a bird's eye view of the Valley of Chevreuse, as well as Château de Versailles and its French gardens. If you've got the cash, it's the ideal way to really get perspective on Paris.

HéliParis: 23 Rue Henri Farman, 75015, +33 1 41 31 33 92. Métro: Balard. Price: 30-minute flight for €139, per person. www.helicoptere.com ⌛

Noodle Around

Although half a century ago you'd only come here if you were in the market for a male prostitute, now **Rue Saint-Anne** is the place to go for a taste of Japan. Lined with Japanese shops and sushi and noodle bars, you won't get far before stopping for a snack. Be prepared to wait, though: most restaurants are tiny and don't take reservations. Get your chopsticks at the ready and join the queue!

Overwhelmed by the choice? Check out **Kunitoraya** (if you can get through the door!) and suck back some udon noodles.

Rue Sainte-Anne: 75001. Métro: Pyramides.

Kunitoraya: 39 Rue Sainte-Anne, 75001, +33 1 47 03 33 65. Métro: Pyramides. Open: daily 11:30 am to 10 pm. www.kunitoraya.com 🍜

Pound the Pavement

If all that fine food is threatening to make you tip the scales, why not combine a little tourism and exercise with **Get in Shape's Footing Touristique**. Choose from a variety of jogging routes ranging from 3 km to 20 km, each taking in a few sights along the way. A guide accompanies you to keep you on track – and to provide a little motivation when your pastry-induced sugar-rush subsides. Get your trainers on and experience Paris with a runner's high.

Footing Touristique: Get in Shape, +33 6 09 47 25 49. 3-km jogging route departs from and returns to Hôtel de Ville, 75004. Métro: Hôtel de Ville. Price: €60 per hour for individual session; €80 per hour for group up to 8 people. www.getinshape.fr ⌛

Fresh Face

Jump-start your preparations for the evening ahead at make-up studio **Gloss'UP.** Using professional Viseart make-up, you can sip a drink as the make-up artists give you a whole new look. Make the most of your eyes with a half-hour session for €30, or learn the basics of make-up application for €60. Whatever you choose, you can be sure you'll emerge from the studio with your game face on.

Gloss'UP: 58 Rue Charlot, 75003, +33 1 09 64 03 23 19. Métro: Filles du Calvaire. Open: Tues to Sat 11 am to 7 pm. www.gloss-up.com

Lord and Master

Named after Paris' first bishop, the church of **Saint Denys du Saint Sacrement** is home to a painting by legendary French artist Eugene Delacroix. A leader in the French Romantic school whose works were copied by Renoir and Manet, Delacroix's creation – depicting Christ's removal from the cross – decorates a small chapel inside the main sanctuary. As well as its artistic claim to fame, the church also boasts an organ dating from 1839. Take a wander though this nineteenth-century place of worship, listen to some age-old music and see a great Master up close.

Saint Denys du Saint Sacrement: 68 bis rue de Turenne, 75003, +33 1 44 54 35 88. Métro: Saint-Sébastien – Froissart or Chemin Vert. Open: daily 8 am to 7 pm (holidays 8 am to 12 pm, 4:30 pm to 7 pm). http://catholique-paris.cef.fr/-632-Saint-Denys-du-Saint-Sacrement-.html

24 Hour Fact

It is customary to attend a dinner party in Paris 15 minutes after the invited time.

18:00

Art for the People

Once a former funeral home run by the state, **104** is now a place where art comes alive. Designed as a venue for art to engage with the public and vice versa, the 39,000 square metre exhibition space has an ever-changing programme of installations, as well as a special children's area for young ones to make their own creations. Eat alongside the artists in the restaurant, shop for your own supplies, and hone your talents in the space for amateurs. There's no rest for the artistic here.

104: 104 Rue d'Aubervilliers and 5 Rue Curiel, 75019, +33 1 53 35 50 00. Métro: Stalingrad, Riquet. Open: Tues to Thurs, Sun 11 am to 8 pm; Fri, Sat 11 am to 11 pm. Price: free. Exhibitions €5; concessions €3. www.104.fr 🎭

Blast from the Past

Looking for your favourite vinyl record from the seventies? An old ghetto blaster or an eighties-style denim vest? Make your way to vintage shop **Aux Comptoir du Chineur**, where you'll find a pleasant mish-mash of slices of life from the 1950s through to the 1980s. This isn't your usual junk shop:

each item is in good condition and you won't need to comb through rails of hideous jumpers and broken bits to find something to take away. From sunglasses to comic books, if you're craving a blast from the past you'll certainly get it here.

Aux Comptoirs du Chineur: 49 Rue Saint Paul, 75004, +33 1 42 72 47 39. Métro: Saint-Paul or Bastille. Open: Tues to Sun 2 pm to 8 pm.

Go Climbing

If you've conquered the Eiffel Tower and the Arc de Triomphe and you're looking for some other heights to scale, head to futuristic La Défense where a giant arch of a different kind awaits. Completed in 1989, the cube-like **Grande Arche de la Défense** echoes the Arc de Triomphe in structure but not in philosophy: it celebrates humanitarian ideologies rather than military conquests.

Located at the end of the *Axe Historique*, the line of monuments running through Paris' core, the glass-covered concrete structure provides a great view of the city centre. Watch office workers scuttle into the surrounding skyscrapers and take in a whole new corporate side to the City of Romance.

Grande Arche de la Défense: 1 Parvis de la Défense, 92044, +33 1 49 07 27 27. Métro: Grande Arche La Défense. Open: daily 10 am to 8 pm (until 7 pm in winter). Price: adult €10, child €8.50. www.grandearche.com

If the Shoe Fits

A trip to Paris would be remiss without a visit to legendary French shoemaker **Christian Louboutin**. His creations – easily recognisable by their crimson soles and killer heels – have been worn by almost every Hollywood star imaginable, from Oprah to Sarah Jessica Parker. Louboutin's designs were influenced by the showgirls of Paris nightclubs he used to skip school to watch. Add a little bit of Paris glamour to your step (if you can manage to walk on the sky-high heels, that is) and teeter about on your own custom-made stilettos from his boutique on Rue Jean-Jacques Rousseau.

Christian Louboutin: 19 Rue Jean-Jacques Rousseau, 75001, +33 1 42 36 53 66. Métro: Palais Royal-Musée du Louvre. Open: Mon to Sat 10:30 am to 7 pm. www.christianlouboutin.com

Marvellous Medal

Join the masses of pilgrims and make your way to one of Paris' most visited sights: the **Chapel of the Miraculous Medal**. In 1830, the Virgin is said to have appeared here to Saint Catherine Labouré – then a sister at the convent – to give the world a medal. Two years later, a deadly cholera epidemic hit Paris. The sisters began distributing medals to stricken Parisians, who then claimed to be miraculously cured. Sink into a pew and take your own rest cure during the chapel's Vespers, held every day but Tuesday at 6:30 pm. And if you want a medal of your own, you can get one from the slot machines on premises.

Chapelle de la Médaille Miraculeuse: Couvent des Soeurs de Saint-Vincent-de-Paul, 140 Rue du Bac, 75007, +33 1 49 54 78 88. Métro: Sèvres-Babylone. Open: daily 7:45 am to 1 pm, 2:30 pm to 7 pm. Price: free. Vespers held at 6:30 pm every day but Tues.
www.chapellenotredamedelamedaillemiraculeuse.com

Bubbly on Board

Champagne on the Seine: you couldn't get a more perfect Parisian way to start the night if you tried. Drift down the river as you sip three kinds of bubbly with **Ô Chateau**'s hour-long boat ride. The *sommelier* will fill you in and top you up, providing information on what you're drinking as well as pointing out the sights from the Eiffel Tower to the Arab World Institute and back. The City of Light never looked – or tasted – so good.

Champagne Cruise: book online at www.o-chateau.com. Cruises available Mon to Sat at 6 pm. Price: €45. ⧗

Skate Away

If you're sick of the sights and you want to see some action of a different kind, you can find it at **Cosanostra Skateboard Park**. Practise your moves on the wide variety of wooden modules, or grab your skateboard and hit the ramps at this 2500-square-metre indoor venue. Don't worry if you don't have your own gear – skateboards and rollerskates (including protection for your wrists, knees and arms!) are available free of charge.

Cosanostra: 18 Rue du Tir, 77500, Chelles, +33 1 64 72 14 04. Métro: RER E Gare de Chelles. Opening hours vary by season but generally open from 2 pm to 8 pm; later during term-time. Check website for details. Price: €6. www.cosanostraskatepark.net

Snack Happy

Scoff some free veggies and dip along with your cocktail at **The Honest Lawyer**. A cross between a bar and a pub, you can watch sports on the plasma screen or down drinks during their daily Happy Hour from 5:30 pm to 8:30 pm. It's not exactly Irish, not exactly French, but if you're looking for somewhere to drink and snack (relatively) cheaply in the pricy sixteenth *arrondissement*, this might be it.

The Honest Lawyer: 176 Rue de la Pompe, 75016, +33 1 45 05 14 23. Métro: Victor Hugo. Open: daily 8 am to 12 am. www.honest-lawyer.com

Leather Master

It's anything but cheap but if you've always hankered after a personalised handbag then leather designer **Serge Amoruso** is your man. After seven years learning from the masters at Hermès, Amoruso decided it was time to strike out on his own. At his shop and studio in the Marais, you can watch artisans at work fashioning his creations from exotic skins and see the finished goods in the shop window next door. Place your order, then watch it take shape.

Serge Amoruso: 13 Rue Abel, 75012, +33 1 43 45 14 10. Métro: Gare de Lyon, Ledru-Rollin. Open: Mon to Fri 11 am to 7 pm (by appointment only). ⌛

Off the Charts

Looking for an authentic Parisian dining experience within budget? Get a taste of old-world elegance at a fraction of the price at **Restaurant Chartier**. Over a hundred years old, the restaurant's changed hands only four times and much of the traditional decor in the cavernous space remains unaltered. Once a soup kitchen for the blue-collar workers of the area, Chartier's menu – and clientele – has evolved but the cheerful and buzzing ambiance remains. With a glass ceiling and mirrors everywhere, you can sneak a peek at your neighbour's food and watch the waiters, dressed in their traditional uniform of black waistcoat and long white apron, bustle around you. Fill your senses and your belly with the Paris of days gone by. Just do it quickly: with diners packed in around you and service that's fast and furious, this is not a place to linger.

Chartier: 7 Rue du Faubourg Montmartre, 75009, +33 1 47 70 86 29. Métro: Grands Boulevards. Open: daily 11:30 am to 3 pm, 6 pm to 10 pm. www.restaurant-chartier.com 🦐

Put on Your Dancing Shoes

Since 1947, ballet shoemaker **Repetto** has fashioned over one million pairs of ballet shoes. Worn by Brigitte Bardot and championed by Serge Gainsbourg, Repetto has made its legendary shoe street-ready by pairing with designers such as Issey Miyake and Commes des Garçons.

Watch the ballerinas twirl to test their new slippers as you search for your own perfect pair. Even Hillary Clinton's a fan!

Repetto: 22 Rue de la Paix, 75002, +33 1 44 71 83 12. Métro: Opéra. Open: Mon to Sat 9:30 am to 7:30 pm. www.repetto.com

News à la Mode

Head to the counter to take your coffee with the journalists at **Café Mode**. Located close to top national radio station Europe 1, this packed café is where those in the know go for their caffeine fix. Grab one of the daily papers on offer, slug back your drink and keep your ears peeled for the day's news.

Café Mode: 24 Rue François 1er, 75008. Métro: Franklin D. Roosevelt or Alma-Marceau. 🐾

On Your Bike

If your feet are sore but you're still craving more, hope on a bike to get up close and personal with Paris streets. With **Fat Tire Bike Tours**, you can cover 13 km by both bike and boat with the minimum of effort.

Watch as dusk falls over the City of Light as you wheel by the Eiffel Tower, sip a (free!) glass of wine as you cruise the Seine, and even get your tongue around an ice-cream at Berthillon. Chances are you've never had a bike-ride so good.

Fat Tire Bike Tours: meet at South Leg of the Eiffel Tower, 75007, +33 1 56 58 10 54. Métro: Bir-Hakeim. Night Tours run from 6 pm (winter) or 7 pm (summer); check website for details. Tours last for 4 hours. Price: adults €28, students €26. http://fattirebiketours.com/paris ⧖

Have a Laugh

It's non-stop laughter – literally – at this bar cum comedy club. With at least three shows every day, you'll be sure to get some good vibes at **Théâtre Popul'Air** – even if all the shows are in French. From stand-up comedy to poetry slams and even children's shows, get a taste of all things funny (and some beer, too, if you fancy). With only 55 seats, be sure to sit in the back if you don't want to be part of the show.

Théâtre Popul'Air: 36 Rue Henri Chevreau, 75020, +33 1 43 36 74 15. Métro: Pyrénées or Couronnes. Open: daily, 2 pm to 12 am. http://theatrepopulair.over-blog.com

Heavy Medal

If signet rings and gold medallions are your thing, head straight to the King of Bling: **Arthus-Bertrand**. Founded in 1803 as an embroidery shop, over the years its expertise evolved to include designing military and ceremonial medals, as well as jewellery. The official supplier of the Grand Chancellery of the Legion of Honour, this legendary shop is worth a visit to ogle its creations even if you're not in the market for a medal.

Arthus-Bertrand: 6 Place Saint-Germain-des-Prés, 75006, +33 1 49 54 72 10. Métro: Saint-Germain-des-Prés. Open: Mon 11 am to 7 pm, Tues to Sat 10:30 am to 7 pm. www.arthus-bertrand.com

Canal Canoodle

It may not be Venice, but Paris' canals are worth taking a trip down too. **Canal Saint-Martin**, stretching for 4.5 kilometres, was ordered by Napoleon I in 1802 to increase Paris' fresh water supply. The inspiration of Alfred Sisley's 1870 painting *View of the Canal Saint-Martin in Paris,* the canal almost fell victim to redevelopment in the 1960s – proposals suggested it be filled in and made a highway. Today, though, the canal and its surrounding areas are bursting with new life as shops, cafés and galleries open up. Explore its rebirth from the source itself with Canauxrama's Canal Saint-Martin Cruise. Navigate through four locks, pass under bridges and enjoy the calm of the tree-lined walkways. It's the ideal way to explore Paris' hidden corners without having to move a muscle.

Canal Saint-Martin Cruise: Canauxrama 75004, +33 1 42 39 15 00. Departure from Bassin de la Villette, 13 Quai de la Loire, 75019. Métro: Jaurès. Arrival at Arsenal Marina, 75004. Métro: Bastille. Departures at 6 pm. From Oct to April, departures by booking only. Cruises last 2 hours. Price: €16 adult; €8:50 child. www.canauxrama.com

24 Hours of Activity

Hit some balls around p15

Explore the urban jungle p29

Get your groove on p31

Cool down on ice p106

Play pétanque p121

Pound the pavement p128

Generate pedal power p136

Stretch body and soul p142

Scale some heights p151

Swim before turning in p156

Roll around the city p175

Take aim p193

19:00

Work Out

Let off some steam at the end of the day with **Urban Nights**. Held every Thursday, these after-work parties start right at seven and carry on till late. Go to the website and sign up for the guest list, then keep your work kit on and head straight for the bar. A light buffet usually gets the night started and lines your belly for the inevitable drinks to follow. Shed the work week and let loose on the dance floor.

Urban Nights: locations vary; check website for details. Price: €20 (€15 with flyer). After-work dress code. www.urban-nights.com

In the Tree-Tops

Head to Parc de la Villette for one of the oddest-shaped clubs with some of the best music you can find in Paris. **Le Trabendo** is located in a 'folie' – a bizarre red building on stilts rising to tree-level – created by architect Bernard Tschumi in the early 1900s.

The club has a long history of hosting musical greats, from Keziah Jones to Manu Chao and even Metallica.

Not a concert hall, not quite a club, with Le Trabendo's surreal structure and fresco-covered walls you'll feel like you've wandered into a strange musical never-never land.

Le Trabendo: Parc de la Villette, 211 Avenue Jean Jaurès, 75018, +33 1 49 25 89 99. Métro: Porte de Pantin. Most concerts start around 7:30 pm; check website for details. Price: tickets from around €20. www.trabendo.fr

Grill and Chill

With summertime BBQs on the roof and interior design by Philippe Starck, you can't go wrong at **Mama Shelter**. This ultra-cool hotel – created by the co-founders of Club Med – offers non-residents the chance to hang out on high or sample delights down below at the two bars and restaurant. Get a taste of how the hip live at one of the 50 most stylish business hotels in the world, according to *Wallpaper* and *Fortune* magazines. And if you want to stay a bit longer, rooms are surprisingly affordable – prices start from around €110 per night.

Mama Shelter: 109 Rue de Bagnolet, 75020, +33 1 43 48 45 45. Métro: Gambetta. Live music from Thurs to Sat. Rooftop BBQ from May. Limited menu available until 1:30 am; brunch every Sun for €39. www.mamashelter.com

To the Point

With a concert hall, dance studios, artists-in-residence and a trendy location on up-and-coming Canal Saint-Martin – not to mention a bar and restaurant – **Point Ephémère** has something for everyone. Located in an old warehouse, the arts centre opened in 2004 and has been a popular port of call ever since. Have a drink on the canal-side terrace or browse the exhibitions by young artists; watch a choreographer work with dancers or take in a concert. At Point Ephémère, you'll feel more cultured just by being there.

Point Ephémère: 200 Quai de Valmy, 75010, +33 1 40 34 02 48; restaurant +33 1 40 34 04 06. Métro: Jaurès or Louis Blanc. Bar open Mon to Sat 12 pm to 2 am; Sun 1 pm to 9 pm. Restaurant open 12 pm to 2:30 pm; 8 pm to 11 pm. www.pointephemere.org

Stretch Your Muscles

With all the culture about in Paris it's easy to stretch your brain, but don't forget about your body! For a little exercise of the physical kind, go to **Red Earth Centre** where Australian Louise Raszyk has drawn upon her extensive training in body well-being to offer up a selection of yoga, flamenco and zen classes. Synch your body with your mind and learn a few new moves at the same time.

Red Earth Centre: 235 Rue La Fayette, 75010, +33 1 40 38 40 52. Métro: Jaurès. Most evening classes start at 7:30 pm; check website for details. Price: trial Yoga class €15; 10-session card €150. www.redearthcentre.com ⧗

Get a Piece of It

If you want to try everything but your eyes are usually bigger than your stomach, never fear: at **Atelier Joël Robuchon**, you can sample tapas-sized classic French dishes without getting too full for more. Crowned 'chef of the century' by foodie guide *Gault Millau*, Robuchon has trained up chefs like Gordon Ramsay and Eric Ripert. One of his three restaurants in Paris, sitting at Atelier's horseshoe-shaped counter you can watch your dishes – and those of your fellow diners – being prepared and delivered.

Perch up high on one of the 36 stools and don't even try to resist.

Atelier Joël Robuchon: 5 Rue Montalembert, 75007, +33 1 42 22 56 56. Métro: Rue du Bac. Open: daily 11:30 am to 3:30 pm, 6:30 pm to 12 am. www.joel-robuchon.com 🍄

Changing Rooms

Make like Superman and get your kit off in a phone booth at **Noir Kennedy**. Here, you can choose from the selection of vintage clothes imported from England and Sweden, then try them on for size in the iconic red British telephone booths that double as changing rooms. So-named due to the co-owner's fascination with the secrets of the Kennedy family, Noir Kennedy is a worth a browse even if you're not in the hunt for a vintage rock T-shirt.

Just watch out for the stuffed rats hanging from the ceiling!

Noir Kennedy: 12 and 22 Rue Du Roi de Sicile, 75004, +33 1 42 71 15 50. Métro: Saint-Paul. Open: Tues to Sat 11 am to 8 pm; Sun 2 pm to 8 pm; Mon 1 pm to 8 pm. www.noirkennedy.fr

Personal Space

If you really want to know the French, there's only one thing for it: breaking bread. With **Meeting the French**, you can choose the French hosts that suit you (and speak your language), then sit down with them in the comfort of their own home and have a meal. The catered meal's on you though; choose your menu and wine from €60 per guest. Hosts receive nothing except the pleasure of interacting with you, so sit back and practise your charm on the masters.

Meeting the French: date and time of your choice. Most hosts located in central Paris. Price: meals from €60 per guest. www.meetingthefrench.com ⌛ 🍽

In the Cabbage Patch

Walking into **Rose et Chou-fleur** (so-named after a French saying that boys are born in the cabbage patch, while girls enter the world via the rose garden) is like opening a treasure chest where everything you ever desired as a child is right there in front of you. From frilly pink princess dresses to glistening jewellery fashioned from semi-precious stones, all that you see is hand-made by creator Zoé d. Pick up a one-off tiara or lampshade and fulfil your childhood dreams.

Rose et Chou-fleur: 34 Rue des Vinaigriers, 75010, +33 1 46 07 78 83. Métro: Jacques Bonsergent. Open: Tues to Sat 11 am to 8 pm; Sun 3 pm to 7 pm. www.rose-et-chou-fleur.com

Go Native

You won't find tourists at **Le Tribal Café**, but you will find a great crowd of natives ready to party. Head down the back alley to the hidden courtyard – make sure to go early to get a table – then follow the locals and dance on top! With mussels or couscous served up for free before 9 pm and plenty of drink on hand, you'll feel right at home.

Le Tribal Café: 3 Cour des Petites Écuries, 75010, + 33 1 47 70 57 08. Métro: Château d'Eau. Open: daily 11 am to 2 am. Free mussels or couscous Wed to Sat evenings up to 9 pm. http://le-tribal-cafe.ifrance.com 🎺

Nice Ice

Paris can get a little chilly around Christmas, but you can warm-up with some on-ice exercise at the **Hôtel de Ville ice-skating rink**. Every year from around mid-December to February, a rink is created outside City Hall. Go at night to marvel at the beautifully lit architecture of the building. Admission is free, but if you don't have your own skates you'll need to pay €5 for a pair.

Ice Skating: Hôtel de Ville, 75004. Métro: Hôtel de Ville. Open: from Dec to Feb, Mon to Thurs 12 pm to 10 pm; Fri 12 pm to 12 am; Sat 9 am to 12 am; Sun 9 am to 10 pm. Price: free, but €5 for skate rental. ⌛ 🚶

On the Water

Take an evening cruise on the Seine at a fraction of the price by hopping on Paris' water shuttle service, **Voguéo**. Stopping at five stations between the Gare d'Austerlitz and the École Vétérinaire de Maisons-Alfort, the catamarans run every 15 to 20 minutes each day of the year. Watch Paris light up from one side to other on the half-hour journey.

Voguéo: weekday services runs every 15 or 20 minutes from around 7 am to 9 pm. Weekend and holiday services runs every 20 minutes from around 10 am to 8:30 pm. Route map and timetable available at www.vogueo.fr. Price: €3 (single ticket).

Sun Kings

If you're after eye-popping performances, get yourself over to an old munitions factory where avant-garde **Le Théâtre du Soleil** will deliver theatre the likes of which you've never seen. Founded in 1964, the ensemble uses unconventional sets and spaces to perform their own creations. Peer behind the curtain as the actors prepare – don't worry, you're allowed! – and get ready for anything.

Make sure to book well in advance: the theatre is extremely popular with Parisians.

Le Théâtre du Soleil: Cartoucherie, Route Champ de Manœuvres, 75012, +33 1 43 74 24 08 (daily from 11 am to 6 pm). Métro: Château de Vincennes, then take the theatre's shuttle bus marked 'Cartoucherie'. Bus starts running 75 minutes before shows. Or take Bus 112 and get off at stop marked 'Cartoucherie'. Show times and prices vary; check website for details. www.theatre-du-soleil.fr ⌛

Get Sketchy

Don't worry if you're not Picasso: at **Dr Sketchy's Anti-Art School**, drawing's only half the fun. With burlesque dancers, fetish models and assorted others standing at the ready to be sketched – and often performing to spice things up – your eyes will be entertained even if you can't get it all down on paper. Started in 2005 in New York City, the concept has now spread to over 80 cities around the world. Bring along your pen and paper and join in the anti-art fun.

Dr Sketchy Anti-Art School: monthly; dates and times vary (drawing usually starts around 7 pm). Check website for details. www.myspace.com/drsketchysaparis ⌛

Wax Poetic

Celebrate literature and interact with Parisian poets at the House of Poetry. Specialising in contemporary poetry, the House offers a variety of film screenings, readings and festivals. Check the website to see what's on, then get ready to divine your own meaning from the torrent of words that flow here.

La Maison de la Poésie: Passage Molière, 157 Rue Saint Martin, 75003, +33 1 44 54 53 00. Métro: Rambuteau. Performance times and prices vary; check website for details. www.maisondelapoesieparis.com ⌛

Mother Tongue

A café and performance venue rolled into one, if you're craving English theatre you can get it at **Le Pavé d'Orsay**. Just minutes from the Museé d'Orsay, this small space frequently performs in English. While the plays may lack a little polish and the sets are very basic, the enthusiasm of the actors more than makes up it. Leave your fledgling French at the door and switch your mind back into English.

Le Pavé d'Orsay: 48 Rue de Lille, 75007, lepavedorsay@gmail.com. Métro: Rue du Bac. Performance times and prices vary; check website for details. http://lepavedorsay.blogspot.com ⌛ 🎭

24 Hours of Food

Head to the market p10

Fill your belly with bread p21

Learn some new kitchen moves p26

Eat as time ticks p51

Cram in some crêpes p63

Have a meal at a mosque p77

Munch on legendary falafel p98

Take tea in luxury p122

Slurp up some noodles p127

BBQ with a view p141

Experience libation in a secret location p152

Devour the best of Breton p157

Eat duck at any hour p172

Ring your bell-y p200

Have a champagne picnic p201

20:00

Ghost Hunt

It may be the City of Light but Paris still has plenty of dark corners to explore. See what secrets lie beneath the city's gilded exterior on the **Paris Ghost Tour**. Learn about serial killers and vampires, Knights Templar and mummies – and more. After poking your nose where the sun doesn't shine, you'll never look at Paris the same way again.

Paris Ghost Tour: meet at Rebel Bar, 10 Rue des Lombards, 75004, +33 9 77 21 82 10. Métro: Châtelet or Hôtel de Ville. Tours run every Fri and Sat at 8 pm for ages 18 and older. Check website for details. Tours last 2.5 hours. Price: €20. www.mysteriesofparis.com ⧗

From Russia with Love

Eat in time to Russian tunes at the simple yet cosy **Cantine Russe** at the Conservatoire Rachmaninoff. Founded in 1923 – with legendary Russian musician Serge Rachmaninoff as the first Honorary President – conservatory students learn Western classical music along with instruction in Roma and Klezmer traditions. The restaurant right below the school offers Russian fare along with a nightly music programme of Russian music. Order some beef stroganoff (the chef's speciality) and escape to another world.

Cantine Russe: Conservatoire Russe de Paris Serge Rachmaninoff, 26 Avenue de New York, 75116, +33 1 47 20 56 12. Métro: Iéna. Restaurant open 12 pm to 2 pm, 8 pm onwards every day but Sun, Mon. Music programme 8 pm to 1:30 am. Price: lunch menu from €17; dinner menu from €32. www.lacantinerusse.com 🦑

Hit the Wall

Get vertical at **MurMur** and really test your fear factor on the large indoor wall, with 1,550 square metres of climbing surface. Located in a vast cavernous building, you have to scale heights just to get to the clubhouse – the timber-frame structure is perched up some stairs in the middle of the hall. Take in the views over the Savoyard chalet and ponder the challenge before you.

MurMur: 55 Rue Cartier-Bresson, 93500, Pantin, +33 1 48 46 11 00. Métro: Aubervilliers-Pantin-Quatre Chemins. Open: Mon to Fri 9:30 am to 11 pm; Sat Sun 9:30 am to 6:30 pm. Price: €8 to €15 (depending on time; check website for details). Joining fee: €15. Rental equipment available. www.murmur.fr

Secret Eats

If you want the thrill of not knowing where your next meal is coming from, log onto **Hidden Kitchen**'s website to sign up for their next secret supper club. Run by two American food consultants, 16 guests are invited into their home for a seasonal ten-course tasting menu (with wine, of course!). You'll receive the secret location information a few days before dinner – then, just turn up for some fine grub in the company of strangers!

Hidden Kitchen: held weekly at 8 pm. Price: €80. www.hkmenus.com ⏳🎥

Floating Film

Ever watched a film whilst floating on a boat? At **La Péniche**, you can take in some cinema and enjoy being aboard a barge at the same time. The barge aims to be a place for new talents to mix with professionals and shows a variety of films from up-and-coming film-makers, as well as experimental cinema. In the summer, the rooftop is the ideal place for tapas and champagne – you can even watch the films by star-light!

And if you want to acquire some skills of your own, La Péniche holds introductory film-making sessions every Wednesday and Saturday afternoons.

La Péniche Cinéma: Canal de l'Ourcq (next to the Cabaret Sauvage), Parc de la Villette, 75019, +33 9 54 73 00 95. Métro: Porte de la Villette. Most shows start at 8:30 pm; check website for details. Tickets: €5. Film-making workshops held every Wed and Sat 2 pm to 5 pm, for children ages 8 to 15. http://penichecinema.net ⌛

Music Mechanics

With three floors, each playing different music from rock and garage to funk and exotica, **La Mécanique Ondulatoire** meets all musical tastes. Head to the cellar for live music or drift through the photo exhibition on the first floor. At this music mecca, you can fill your ears with sweet (or not-so-sweet) sounds for hours.

La Mécanique Ondulatoire: 8 Passage Thiéré, 75011, +33 1 43 55 16 74. Métro: Bastille, Ledru-Rollin, Voltaire. Open: Mon to Sat 6 pm to 2 am. www.lamecond.com

French Funnies

It doesn't really matter if you can't speak the language; at the theatre **Comédie-Française**, you'll feel like you're a part of French history just by being here. Founded in 1680 thanks to a decree from Louis XIV, it's the world's oldest surviving national theatre and continues to be a vibrant part of theatrical society.

With legends like Mlle Clairon and Sarah Bernhardt having graced its stage and a hefty repertoire of comedic classics from Molière and Racine to draw on, you can bet it'll be around for another three centuries, at least.

Comédie-Francaise: Salle Richelieu, 2 Place Colette, 75001, +33 1 44 58 15 15. Métro: Palais Royal-Musée du Louvre. Box office open daily 11 am to 6 pm. Evening performance usually at 8:30 pm; check website for details. Price: tickets from €11 to €37. Go one hour before show for €5 seats. Free for under 28s on Mon. www.comedie-francaise.fr

Purpose Built

If you're looking for a full-on rock concert, head to the **Zénith** in Parc de la Villette. Designed by the Ministry of Culture specifically for rock concerts, after 25 years the Zénith is still going strong. Musical acts like Placebo, Arctic Monkeys and Motorhead have all played here – it was even The Cure's chosen recording location for their album *Paris*. In fact, the rock-hall concept was so successful that 16 other Zéniths opened across France. Come see the one that started the rock ball rolling and listen to some great music at the same time.

Le Zénith de Paris: 211 Avenue Jean Jaurès, 75019. Métro: Porte de la Villette, Porte de Pantin. Book Online. Most concerts start around 8 pm; doors open 90 minutes before show. Ticket prices vary depending on act; check website for details. www.zenith-paris.com.

Dance Inspiration

Take in some of Paris' best cabaret then hit the dance floor yourself at **Bobino**. After the dinner and show – complete with the prerequisite dancers, illusionists and other spectacles – the venue transforms into a heaving nightclub with DJs and strobe lights. Although Bobino is relatively new itself, a club has existed at this location since 1873; Edith Piaf and Josephine Baker are both said to have performed here. Get some dance inspiration and join the ghosts of the past on the dance floor.

Bobino: 14-20 Rue de la Gaîté, 75014, +33 1 43 27 24 24. Métro: Gaîté, Edgar Quinet. Most shows start at 8 pm; doors open one hour before performance. Club from around 11 pm. Tickets from €10 to €70; check website for details. www.bobino.fr ⧗

Nectar of the Gods

Pay homage to the prophetess Sybil at her temple, perched atop a 30-metre-high rocky outcrop at **Buttes Chaumont Park**. You'll have to work to get there: built in 1869, it sits on the edge of an island reachable only by crossing a 63-metre-long suspension bridge on one side, and a 22-metre-high bridge on the other. If you don't feel like playing Indiana Jones, just chill in the 61-acre park (Paris' steepest!) and enjoy the great views over the Sacré Coeur.

If a libation is in order, head through the park to **Rosa Bonheur** for drinks and food in a convivial atmosphere. Named after the old tavern on site when the park was a limestone quarry, you can munch on generous meat platters and seek divine inspiration from the wide selection of wines. With a large terrace and great views, you couldn't conjure up a better place to watch the sun set even if you were Sybil herself.

Parc des Buttes Chaumont: Métro: Buttes Chaumont. Open: daily 7 am to 10 pm (summer); 7 am to 8 pm (winter). Price: free. http://butteschaumont.free.fr 👫

Rosa Bonheur: Parc des Buttes Chaumont, 2 Allée de la Cascade, 75019, +33 1 42 03 28 67. Métro: Botzaris, Buttes Chaumont. Open: Wed to Sat 12 pm to 1:30 pm, 8 pm to 9:30 pm, Sun 12 pm to 5 pm; late nights Fri to Sat until 12 am and beyond (access from gates at 74 Rue Botzaris). www.myspace.com/rosabonheurparis 🍹

Swim under the Stars

There's nothing like a swim before turning in to make you sleep like a baby. Open until 10 pm on Tuesdays and Thursdays, at **Georges Vallerey Pool** you can swim laps till late. With a retractable plexiglass roof, you can even gaze at the stars while you practise your back-crawl.

Named after the French swimmer who won bronze in the 1948 Olympics, this is one of the only 50-metre pools in Paris. Suit up and dive in.

Georges Vallerey Pool: 148 Avenue Gambetta, 75020, +33 1 40 31 15 20. Métro: Porte des Lilas, Saint-Fargeau. Open: Mon 11:45 am to 1:30 pm; Tues, Thurs 11:45 am to 1:30 pm, 5:15 pm to 10 pm; Wed 10 am to 1 pm, 2 pm to 7 pm; Fri 7 am to 6 pm; Sat, Sun 9 am to 5 pm. Hours vary during holidays; check website for details. Price: €2.60; €1.50 concessions. www.paris.fr

Best of Breton

Tucked away off the busy streets and cheaper than sibling restaurant Chez Michel, **Chez Casimir** provides simple yet flavourful bistro fare from chef Thierry Breton's native Brittany. Just minutes from the Gare du Nord, it's the ideal welcome – or farewell – to some great French cooking. Grab a seat at the sturdy wooden tables and get ready to taste the best of Breton, from cockles to oxtail.

Chez Casimir: 6 Rue de Belzunce, 75010, +33 1 48 78 28 80. Métro: Gare du Nord. Open: Mon to Fri 12 pm to 2 pm, 7:30 pm to 11 pm (hours may vary, call ahead before going). ⌛ 🍷

Bread before Bed

If you're craving a baguette before bedtime, seek out **Arnaud Delmontel** for your fix. Winner of the best baguette in Paris in 2007, pastry chef Delmontel first opened shop in 1999 in a fitting location: the site of an old bakery, founded in 1875. Rekindling the spirit of traditional breads and pastries, you can feast on a variety of delights then hit the sack to sleep it off. If it's good enough for Sarkozy (Delmontel is a supplier to the French president), then it's surely good enough for you.

Arnaud Delmontel: 39 Rue des Martyrs, 75009, +33 1 48 78 29 33. Métro: Pigalle, Saint-Georges. Open: daily (except Tues) 7 am to 8:30 pm. www.arnaud-delmontel.com 🦑 👫

Suck it Up

Put aside your dignity and get ready for an experience unlike any other. At **Le Refuge des Fondues**, you'll share your table with other diners, scribble on walls and suck wine from a baby bottle.

It may sound like dining hell, but the convivial atmosphere and packed-like-sardines benches mean you can talk to just about anyone. Get your fill of fondue and enjoy your alcoholic oral fixation!

Le Refuge des Fondues: 17 Rue des Trois Frères, 75018, +33 1 42 55 22 65. Métro: Abbesses. Open: daily 7 pm to 12 pm. 🦑

Sing for Your Supper

Eat your dinner while you're serenaded by the very people serving it up. At **Bel Canto**, the waiters double as opera singers who pause between courses to treat you to classics from Rossini and Mozart, to name a few. Here, every mouthful you take will taste that much better with the sweet sounds of opera swirling around you. Sip a glass from the extensive wine list and let your senses soak it all in.

Bel Canto: 72 Quai de l'Hôtel de Ville, 75004, +33 1 42 78 30 18. Métro: Pont Marie or Hôtel de Ville. Reservations for 8 pm, 8:30 pm and 9 pm. Price: set menu €76. www.lebelcanto.com ⏳ 🦐

Goose Bumps

Cool things down at the **Ice Kube**, a bar where everything's made of ice – even the glass your drink's served in! Pull on your parka and perch on an armchair fashioned from icy blocks as the Grey Goose vodka (included in your price of admission) lights up your insides. Located inside the equally cool Hotel Kube, you'll emerge from the experience ready to heat things up again.

Ice Kube: Hotel Kube, 1-5 Passage Ruelle, 75018, +33 1 42 05 2000. Métro: La Chapelle. Open: Wed to Sat 7 pm to 1:30 am, Sun 2 pm to 11 pm. Price: €38 for 30 mins. http://90plan.ovh.net/~kubehote ⏳

Dance Down Under

Craving a raucous good time away from the elegant confines of Parisian bars? Head over to **Café Oz,** where you couldn't be further from Paris if you tried. Decorated with the typical Aussie icons of kangaroos and crocodiles, the mix of globe-trotters, expats and anyone else ready to party 'til late means a good time here is practically guaranteed. Grab a Foster's from the Antipodean bar staff, watch some sport or groove on a table-top. You might be miles from Australia but you'll definitely feel at home!

Café Oz: 18 Rue Saint-Denis, 75001, +33 1 40 39 00 18. Métro: Châtelet. Open: Sun to Wed 5 pm to 3 am, Thurs 5 pm to 4 am, Fri 5 pm to 6 am, Sat 1 pm to 6 am. www.cafe-oz.com

Happy Hang-Out

Fittingly located on the 'Street of Laughs', you can't help but enjoy yourself at **Les Trois Arts**. Peruse the artist exhibitions as you sip your coffee, play a game of chess and browse the library, then head to the cellar for the night's main event. Showcasing anything from world music and jazz to story-telling and improv games, Les Trois Arts' varied programme will certainly keep you on your toes.

Les Trois Arts: 21 Rue des Rigoles, 75020, +33 1 43 49 36 27. Métro: Jourdain or Gambetta. Open: Tues to Sun 5 pm to 2 am. http://les3arts.free.fr

21:00

Sing-a-Long

Rough and ready, **Le Vieux Belleville** gives you a taste of old-school Paris. Go on Thursdays and Fridays for the accordion sing-a-longs, where musicians give you a song book to join in with the locals who frequently pack the place out. If you want to put more than words in your mouth, you can enjoy the traditional bistro fare on offer. Fill your belly then sing like a bird.

Le Vieux Belleville: 12 Rue des Envierges, 75020, +33 1 44 62 92 66. Métro: Pyrénées. Sing-a-longs held Thurs to Sat from 9 pm to 2 am. Restaurant open Mon to Fri from 11 am to 3 pm; Thurs to Sat from 8 pm to 2 am. www.le-vieux-belleville.com 🎤

Meeting of Minds

Get a little intellectual stimulation with your evening meal at **Le Lieu Dit**. With a monthly film club, a literary café featuring frequent author reading and events, and an ever-changing programme of visual arts exhibitions, this is the place to satisfy your mind as well as your appetite. Check the website to see what's on, then drop in to join the lively debates.

Le Lieu Dit: 6 Rue Sorbier, 75020, +33 1 40 33 26 29. Métro: Ménilmontant, Gambetta. Open: daily (except Monday) 5 pm to 2 am. Restaurant open daily 6 pm to 12 am. www.lelieudit.com 🎥

Mane Event

Want a new tribal hairdo, complete with braids and feather-like tufts? From super-long hair extensions to radical colours, if you're looking for a brave new look then hit **Space Hair**. Opened in 1996, its star-covered interior with booming music was more like a dance-club than a hair salon – and Parisians loved it.

Although it's somewhat tamer now, it still retains its alternative feeling with trendy haircuts custom-designed for the young clientele who flock through the doors.

Open until late, you can get your new 'do then head straight to a club without losing much party time.

Space Hair: 8-10 Rue Rambuteau, 75003, +33 1 48 87 28 51. Métro: Rambuteau. Open: Mon 12 pm to 10 pm; Tues to Sat 10 am to 10 pm; Sun 11:30 am to 8 pm. Price: cuts starting from €18. Booking advised. www.space-hair.com

On the Roof

Filled with greenery and out in the open, the roof-top terrace at **La Bellevilloise** is a great place to clear your head before the evening kicks off. The first artistic co-operative in Paris, La Bellevilloise was created in 1877 to bring art and culture to the people. With a screening room, night club and a jam-packed schedule of events, you won't have to go far to get the night started.

La Bellevilloise: 19-21 Rue Boyer, 75020, +33 1 46 36 07 07. Métro: Gambetta. Open: Wed, Thurs 7 pm to 2 am; Fri 6 pm to 2 am; Sat 11 am to 2 am; Sun 11 am to 1 am. Terrace open Wed, Thurs 7 pm to 11 pm; Fri 6 pm to 11 pm; Sat 11 am to 11 pm; Sun 11 am to 11 pm. www.labellevilloise.com

Vine and Wine

It's not very auspicious looking, but the small patch of land on the corner of Rue des Saules and Rue Saint-Vincent – way off Montmartre's tourist track – is actually a working vineyard, Paris' last. Montmartre's hills were once the prime location for vineyards as far back as the twelfth century, but real-estate developers gradually took over as Paris' population grew. To preserve the heritage of the area, a group of artists saved a plot of land and proposed a vineyard. In 1934, the first grapes were harvested.

Today, **Clos Montmartre Vineyard** grows 27 varieties of grapes on 1500 square metres, producing 1500 bottles annually sold off in charity auctions. Getting inside the vineyard to have a look (and taste) is difficult, but if you're around in October you can get your fill at the annual harvest festival.

If all those vines have whet your appetite, head over to nearby **Au Lapin Agile**. Featured in Picasso's 1905 painting, this cabaret was originally named Cabaret des Assassins after the owner's son was murdered here. Its colourful history continued despite the change of name, and over the years it's been frequented by artists, pimps, students and upper-class punters looking to slum it for the night. Today the cabaret is more popular with tourists than eccentrics, but it's still fun to sing along to French classics from the fifteenth century to Edith Piaf – even if you can't understand the words (be warned: the whole show is in French).

Clos Montmartre: corner of Rue des Saules and Rue Saint-Vincent, 75018. Métro: Lamarck-Caulaincourt. Harvest festival held each October. Check festival website for details. www.fetedesvendangesdemontmartre.com ⌛

Au Lapin Agile: 22 Rue des Saules, 75018, +33 1 46 06 85 87. Métro: Lamarck-Caulaincourt. Open: Tues to Sun 9 pm to 2 am. Price: €24; student €17 (except on Sat). Price includes one free drink. Reservations recommended. www.au-lapin-agile.com

Party On Board

In the summer, the plant-packed top deck of **Bateau El-Alamein** is ideal for enjoying the last rays of *le soleil*. But all year round, this boat's the perfect place to watch some great live acts. The narrow confines of the lower deck (doubling as a concert hall) lets you get up close to the contemporary bands that play here, while the eccentric decor of mirrors, bright teal walls and various other random objects adds to the feeling that you're miles from the city. Get on board and let the music sail you away.

Bateau El-Alamein: Quai François Mauriac (in front of Bibliothèque François Mitterrand), 75013. Métro: Quai de la Gare. Concert times and ticket prices vary; check website. http://elalamein.free.fr

Get Some Spirit

To get more soul(s), call on the undead to join the party every third Thursday of the month at **Paris Paranormal**. Held less than 50 metres from Père Lachaise Cemetery, the séance aims to speak with those who have crossed to the other side. It's all in French, but what's a little language barrier when it comes to spectral communication?

Paris Paranormal: 52 Rue des Rondeaux, 75020, +33 6 31 38 37 62. Métro: Gambetta. Held every third Thursday of the month from 8 pm to 10:30 pm. www.lesjeudisduparanormal.fr ⌛

Just Jazz

Down a modest street and through a slightly battered door, there's no pretention at jazz club **New Morning**. You get just what you came for: great music. Go early to score a stage-side seat (you won't be able to grove later as people pack the place in) and move whatever body-parts you can to the funky beat. In this no-frills establishment, the music really is the star.

New Morning: 7-9 Rue des Petites-Écuries, 75010, +33 1 45 23 51 41. Métro: Château d'Eau. Most concerts start at 9 pm; check website for details. Ticket prices vary. www.newmorning.com ⏳

Past Pleasures

It may be slightly kitsch, but who cares when you're having this much fun. Relive the spirit of the past at **Nos Anĉetres Les Gaulois** with an all-you-can-eat salad buffet, steaks grilled in the fireplace and wine poured straight from barrels.

The restaurant occupies five different sixteenth and seventeenth-century buildings, gradually knocked together as its popularity grew. With rough stone walls covered in animal skins and a cave-like atmosphere, you'll definitely get that Gallic feeling. Let the wandering troubadours entertain you with traditional tunes as you feast.

Nos Ançetres Les Gaulois: 39 Rue Saint-Louis-en-l'Île, 75004, +33 1 46 33 66 07. Métro: Pont Marie. Open: daily 7 pm to 2 am. Booking recommended. Price: set menu (including all-you-can drink wine) €41. www.nosancetreslesgaulois.com 🦐

Eat in the Tub

If you've always wanted to munch in the bath-tub, now's your chance. At **Les Bains Douches,** located in a former Turkish bath-house once frequented by the likes of Marcel Proust, you can fill your belly to your heart's content without getting scolded. Order up some tempura or other Japanese delights then dance it off at the late-night club. Just be sure to put on your best bath-time outfit: this hot-spot is popular with Paris' in-crowd and to make it through the door you've got to look the part.

Les Bains Douches: 7 Rue du Bourg-l'Abbé, 75003, +33 1 53 01 40 60. Métro: Étienne Marcel. Restaurant open Wed to Sun 8 pm to 1 am. Club open Wed to Sun 12 am to 6 am. Club cover charge: €10 to €20. www.lesbainsdouches.net 🦐

Exotic Dancers

Mix it up Indian style every Friday and Saturday night at **Bollywood Lounge**, where Indian DJs hit the decks with the eclectic 'electro lounge Bollywood'. Get out on the floor and practise your more exotic moves, then head upstairs to the restaurant to re-energise with masala, the house speciality. Light your mouth on fire with some spice then go back down to burn up the dance floor.

Bollywood Lounge: 57 Rue Galande, 75005, +33 1 43 26 25 26. Métro: Maubert-Mutualité or Cluny – La Sorbonne. Restaurant open daily from 12 pm to 2:30 pm and 7 pm to 11:30 pm. Club every Fri and Sat night after 9 pm. www.bollywoodloungeparis.com 🦐

Celebrate Curves

Take a walk on the wild side and cross the curvy pedestrian bridge linking Bercy with the Bibliothèque Nationale. The last bridge on the Seine, the **Passerelle Simone de Beauvoir** was constructed of metal in Alsace and brought by barge to Paris, where it was put in place in 2006. Named in honour of one of France's best-loved novelists, the bridge's unconventional structure is a fitting tribute to a writer who was well ahead of her time.

Passerelle Simone de Beauvoir: in front of the Bibliothèque Nationale de France, between Quai François Mauriac, 75013, and Quai de Bercy, 75012. Métro: Quai de la Gare or Bibliothèque François Mitterrand. Open: daily, 24 hours.

24 Hours for 20-somethings

22:00

Go Crazy

Claiming to be 'the most avant-garde cabaret in Paris,' **Crazy Horse** opened in 1951 and is still going strong. With the on-stage nude dancers virtually indistinguishable from each other – only those with perfectly matching bodies are chosen – you'll think your eyes have deceived you. Dita Von Teese, Carmen Electra and Pamela Anderson have all performed here, too. More intimate and less staged than the bigger cabarets, you can get your fill of bouncing breasts but you'll certainly pay for the privilege. Ask to sit at the bar for a cheaper ticket price.

Crazy Horse: 12 Avenue George V, 75008, +33 1 47 23 32 32. Métro: Alma Marceau or George V. Shows on Sun to Fri at 8:15 pm and 10:45 pm; Sat at 7 pm, 9:30 pm and 11:45 pm. www.lecrazyhorseparis.com ⏳

The Underworld

Make like a mermaid and float around to some underwater tunes at **Piscine Pontoise**. Constructed in the 1930s, this Art

Deco pool in the Latin Quarter broadcasts music underwater and is open until late most nights of the week. With private locker cabins, a sauna and access to cardio rooms, you can work off the excesses of the day then let your worries drift away as you swim under the glass roof.

Piscine Pontoise: 19 Rue de Pontoise, 75005, +33 1 55 42 77 88. Métro: Maubert-Mutualité. Open Mon 7 am to 8:30 am, 12:15 pm to 1:30 pm, 4:30 pm to 8 pm; Tues, Thurs 7 am to 8:30 am, 12:15 pm to 1:30 pm, 4:30 pm to 7 pm; Wed 7 am to 8:30 am, 11:30 am to 7:30 pm; Fri 7 am to 8:30 am, 12:15 pm to 1:30 pm, 4:30 pm to 8 pm; Sat 10 am to 7 pm; Sun 8 am to 7 pm. Price: €4.20; €2.40 concessions. Open late: Mon to Wed 8:15 pm to 11:45 pm, Thurs 9 pm to 11:45 pm, Fri 8:15 pm to 11:45 pm. Night price: €10. www.clubquartierlatin.com

Horror Show

If you just can't get enough of cult classic film *The Rocky Horror Picture Show*, **Studio Galande** is the cinema for you. Every Friday and Saturday nights, the place is packed with punters ready for the ritual of throwing rice, toilet rolls and water at the screen – and, by default, the audience. As the only remaining European cinema to regularly show the film, this small single-screen venue has become something of a legend in its own right. Bring along your props, cover up with old clothes, and get ready to sing along.

Studio Galande: 42 Rue Galande, 75005, +33 1 43 54 72 71. Métro: Saint-Michel, Maubert-Mutualité. The Rocky Horror Picture Show screened every Fri and Sat at 10:10 pm. Price: €8. www.studiogalande.fr ⧗

It Takes Two

For a tango or two, head to gay-friendly **La Boîte à Frissons** where men dance with men, women with women, and everyone mixes to a variety of music from traditional accordion to salsa. Friday and Saturday nights kick off with a polka or waltz, then morph into discos where dancers really let loose. Learn some new moves in the company of strangers then hit the floor to make friends.

Tango at La Boîte à Frissons: 13 Rue au Maire, 75003, +33 1 42 72 17 78. Métro: Arts et Métiers. Tango held every Fri and Sat from 10:30 pm. Price: €8. www.boite-a-frissons.fr

Eat Like a Duck

It's duck all day – and night – at restaurant **Petit Carnard** (Little Duck). Almost every dish on the menu features meat straight from the family farm in Haute-Savoie. From duck confit to duck sausage, the food at this warm and cosy restaurant will reassure even the most hardened vegetarian that no duck has died in vain.

Petit Carnard: 19 Rue Henri Monnier, 75009, +33 1 49 70 07 95. Métro: Pigalle or Saint-Georges. Open: daily 7 pm to 12 am. www.resto-lepetitcanard.com

Born Again

Rising from the ashes of a fire which destroyed it in 2004, the historic **Nouvelle Athènes** has been brought back to life as a modern jazz lounge, café and restaurant. Previous incarnations include an artists' cafe (Degas even painted *L'Absinthe* here in 1875); a striptease club for Nazis; and a rock venue. Feel the weight of history and groove to some blues (played on the resident Fazioli grand piano) in this spacious venue.

Nouvelle Athènes: 9 Place Pigalle, 75009, +33 1 49 70 03 99. Métro: Pigalle. Open: Mon to Sat 10:30 am to 2 am. Jazz every Wed to Sat starting at 11 pm. Price: varies, for details: http://lanouvelleathenes.eresto.net

24 Hour Fact
Every building in central Paris is supposedly a mere 500 metres from a métro station.

Out of Sight

If you care more about taste than presentation – or if you just want to try something different for dinner – head to **Dans Le Noir**, where what's on your plate will only be determined by your tastebuds. Based on the theory that without one sense all the others are heightened, you'll dine in complete darkness. Let the blind waiters guide you through the two- or three-course set meal and see if it really is better to be kept in the dark.

Dans Le Noir: 51 Rue Quincampoix, 75004, +33 1 42 77 98 04. Métro: Étienne Marcel or Rambuteau. Open: lunch Sat 12:30 pm; Sun 12 pm; dinner Mon to Sat 7:45 pm or 8:15 pm; 10 pm or 10:30 pm. Dinner on Sunday at 7:45 pm or 9:15 pm. Price: set menu from €39. www.danslenoir.com 🦑

French Funnies

Started by a group of friends in 1969, **Café de la Gare** is the place to go if you're in the mood for some fun – or funnies. With over 300 seats and shows ranging from fringe to stand-up comics to revue, you never know quite what you're in for. It's all in French, but some of the shows are so out there even understanding the language isn't much help. Prepare to be perplexed, entertained and amused all in one go.

Café de la Gare: 41 Rue du Temple, 75004, +33 1 42 78 52 51. Métro: Hôtel de Ville. Varying times; late show usually at 10 pm. Check website for details. Price: from €20. www.cdlg.org ⌛

Get Your Skates On

It's a great way to see the night lights and get some exercise at the same time. The weekly Friday night skate with **Pari Roller** covers 25 km of city streets in just three hours. With ten- to twenty-thousand people along for the ride, police and volunteers keep things moving on the ever-changing route. It's a fun, friendly (and free!) way to get to know the city. Just learn how to stop, then lace up your rollerblades and let the good times roll.

Friday Night Skate: Pari Roller, Tour Montparnasse (Place Raoul Dautry), 75015. Métro: Montparnasse-Bienvenue. Skate held every Friday at 10 pm. Check website for weather-related cancellations. Price: free. www.pari-roller.com. ⌛

Veggie Heaven

Veggies never tasted so good. At **Macéo**, chef Thierry Bourbonnais has created an ever-changing 'Green Menu' using fresh seasonal produce. For €32, you can have a three-course menu *sans* meat, including concoctions like fig-roasted sweet potatoes with coconut emulsion. And if you're accompanied by eaters of meat persuasion, never fear: there are plenty of carcasses for them to munch on, too.

Macéo: 15 Rue des Petits Champs, 75001, +33 1 42 97 53 85. Métro: Pyramides. Open: Mon to Fri 12 pm to 2:30 pm, 7:30 pm to 11 pm; Sat 7:30 pm to 11 pm. Price: three-course set menu for €32. www.maceorestaurant.com 🍤

Chamber Music

Housed in a twelfth-century prison complete with a guillotine that served its purpose well, **Le Caveau des Oubliettes** is a night-spot with ambiance to spare. Grab a drink in the pub upstairs then head down to the caveau – which used to be linked to a nearby prison by underground tunnels – for some free jazz. Today, the sweet sounds of music echo around the small room but centuries ago the room reverberated with the screams of tortured prisoners. Keep your head and avoid the rush down the narrow stairs by getting there at least thirty minutes before the music begins.

Le Caveau des Oubliettes: 52 Rue Galande, 75005, +33 1 46 34 23 09. Métro: Saint Michel or Cluny–La Sorbonne. Open: daily 5 pm to 4 am. Live music from 10 pm (cover charge may be requested on Fri and Sat; otherwise free if you spend at least €6 on drinks). www.caveaudesoubliettes.fr

24 Hours of Culture

Pay homage to a famous Parisienne p11

See Picasso's stomping ground p15

Take in a mini-me Liberty p26

Eyeball the world's archives p50

Get inside the mind of a genius p90

Check out unicorn porn p75

Weave some history p95

See a screen with a past p103

Put the world in focus p113

Head to Hugo's house p115

Check out twin cinemas p122

Get the point p142

Make your eyes pop p146

Have a drink with Hemingway p182

Break some breakfast bread at the cinema p186

23:00

Experimental Experience

It's always cocktail time at the **Experimental Cocktail Club**. From the exposed bricks to the black sofas, this tiny bar in the Montorgueil district oozes speakeasy cool. With live DJs and no shortage of beautiful people packing the narrow confines, all you need to complete the picture is a vodka or champagne concoction. Then lean back and let the night fade away.

Experimental Cocktail Club: 37 Rue St-Sauveur, 75002, +33 1 45 08 88 09. Métro: Sentier, Réaumur-Sébastopol. Open: Mon to Thurs 6 pm to 2 am; Fri to Sat 6 pm to 5 am. www.myspace.com/experimentalcocktailclub

Sing it!

If you've had it with DJs and you prefer to dance to a tune of your own making, head to **L'Enchanteur** for a spot of karaoke. At this gay-friendly cellar bar, you can choose from over 7,000 songs and sing your heart out until morning. And if you really want to get in the game, get here early on Wednesdays for a varied programme of spicy delights to warm up your vocals.

L'Enchanteur: 15 Rue Michel Le Comte, 75003, +33 1 48 04 02 38. Métro: Rambuteau. Open: Tues to Sat 6 pm to 5 am. Karaoke from 10 pm (from 8 pm on Sun); 'One Shot' every Wed from 8 pm. www.lenchanteur-bar.fr

Lounge Lizard

The outdoors comes in at **Lounge Pershing**. Sweep through the lush vertical garden – surrounding you with the scents of over 300 plants – and into a den bathed in pastel light from Murano glass chandeliers. Designed by Andrée Putman, it ain't cheap but it's certainly pretty. Sit back, eek out your pricey drink, and watch the creatures of the night come to life.

Lounge Pershing: Hotel Pershing Hall, 49 Rue Pierre Charron, 75008, +33 1 58 36 58 00. Métro: George V. Open: 6 pm to 2 am daily. www.pershinghall.com

Night Lights

Admire the city on high – 34 floors up, to be exact – at the **Panoramic Bar** in Hotel Concorde La Fayette. With a direct view of the Eiffel Tower and floor-to-ceiling windows to take it all in, you can't get a better view of the City of Light at night. Slither onto a leather banquette and enjoy the show.

Panoramic Bar: Hotel Concorde La Fayette, 3 Place du Général Kœnig, 75017, +33 1 40 68 50 68. Métro: Porte Maillot. Open: Sun to Wed 5 pm to 1:30 am, Thurs to Sat 5 pm to 2:30 am. www.concorde-lafayette.com

King Kong

Designed by Philippe Starck, **Kong** describes itself as the 'fight between the Moderns and the Classics'. While you may never figure out exactly what that means, this bar and restaurant – featured in *Sex and the City* – is worth a visit for its unique design elements such as 'epidermic tables' and 'one-armed chairs', not to mention the great view over the Pont Neuf. Spread over two floors at the top of the Kenzo headquarters, after 10 pm the fifth floor becomes a bar where you can vote for the music you want to hear.

Kong: 1 Rue du Pont Neuf, 75001, +33 1 40 39 09 00. Métro: Pont Neuf. Open: daily 10:30 am to 2 am. www.kong.fr

You Gotta Have Faith

Pay penance for all the drink you've been consuming at **Le Lèche-Vin** (literally, the 'lick wine'). Here, you can have your drink and say some Hail Mary's at the same time. The walls of this student-friendly (read: cheap) drinking den are covered with religious relics, perhaps to atone for the bawdy loos plastered with porn. One look at the rustic Turkish toilets will have even the most hardened sinner begging for deliverance.

Le Lèche-Vin: 13 Rue Daval, 75011, +33 1 43 44 98 91. Métro: Bréguet-Sabin, Bastille. Open: Mon to Thurs 6:30 pm to 1:30 am; Fri, Sat 6 pm to 2 am; Sun 6 pm to 12 am.

Lofty Ideals

Spread out over two levels, Bastille loft **l'OPA** hosts rock, jazz and electro concerts in the evening before morphing into a buzzing club at night. Stretch out on the mezzanine sofas to watch the crowds below you, or take in the video projections on the giant screen. It's trendy, it's free, and it's the ideal way to get an eyeful of Paris life without paying through the nose.

L'OPA Bastille: 9 Rue Biscornet, 75012, +33 1 46 28 12 90. Métro: Bastille (exit Rue de Lyon). Open: concerts held Wed and Thurs from 8 pm; Fri and Sat from 9 pm. Club on Fri and Sat 12 am until dawn. Price: free. www.opa-paris.com

Pick-up Post

If you're a writer without a post box and you want to get your mail along with a cocktail or two, do what Ernest Hemingway did: head to The Ritz. In keeping with tradition, writers can have their post addressed to this iconic hotel. Grab your letters, then order Hemingway's favourite drink – a single-malt whiskey – at the aptly-named **Bar Hemingway**.

Whet your appetite with the 25 photos he took as inspiration for his book *A Moveable Feast* and savour the cocktails prepared by Colin Field, voted the world's best bartender in 2001. Or sip a Bloody Mary, said to have been created so Hemingway's fourth wife, Mary, wouldn't be able to smell alcohol on his breath. Whatever your passion, there's plenty of ways to find stimulation here.

Bar Hemingway: The Ritz Hotel Paris, 15 Place Vendôme, 75001, +33 1 43 16 33 65. Métro: Opéra, Madeleine, Pyramides. Open: daily 10:30 am to 2 am. Semi-formal dress requested. www.ritzparis.com

Rock It

If you're looking for real rock n' roll, then you can't go wrong at **Le Piano Vache**. Just minutes from the Pantheon, this bar is a mecca for students seeking a gritty good time – as well as celebs like Johnny Depp. With aging posters and forgotten student IDs decorating the walls and music from punk to metal, it couldn't be further from Paris' plethora of chi-chi cocktail joints if it tried. Check the website to see what's on (different nights feature different music), put on your downmarket gear and get ready to party!

Le Piano Vache: 8 Rue Laplace, 75005, + 33 1 46 33 75 03. Métro: Maubert-Mutualité or Cardinal Lemoine. Open: Mon to Fri 12 pm to 2 am, Sat 6 pm to 2 am. www.lepianovache.com

Step Back

Said to be the oldest night-club in Paris, **La Java**'s faded glamour is now home to a mix of late-night partiers who come for the live music on the weekends and world music during the week. Edith Piaf and Djano Reinhardt played here during the club's hey-day, and if you block out the modern stylings of ska and rock you can almost still picture it. Get on the dance floor and bust a move in memory of the club's past musical greats.

La Java: 105 Rue du Faubourg du Temple, 75010, +33 1 42 02 20 50. Métro: Belleville or Goncourt. Open: Wed, Thurs 9 pm to 3 am; Fri, Sat 11 pm to 6 am; Sun 2 pm to 2 am. Price: cover charge varies depending on night, usually around €5 to €10. www.la-java.fr

Rooms with a View

Don't expect everything to make sense at **L'Imprévu Café**; in fact, don't expect anything! The very name of this café means 'unpredictable', and one look at its whimsical and quirky interior tips you off to the fact that this is indeed a place like no other. Sit in a barber's chair to take your tea, or head downstairs to the cellar to really get away from it all. Whichever one of its uniquely decorated rooms you choose to hang out in, there's one thing you can predict: you'll feel right at home.

L'Imprévu Café: 9 Rue Quincampoix, 75004, +33 1 42 78 23 50. Métro: Châtelet. Open: daily 3 pm to 2 am (may close earlier on Sundays). www.imprevu-cafe.com

24 Hour Fact
When you rent the Vélib rent-a-bike in Paris, the first 30 minutes are free.

24 Hours of Fear

See if the city's on the brink of destruction p12

Lose your head with market mania p28

Shiver in an infamous prison p39

Check out the original Goth – and some body parts p46

Divine some signs at a mystical tower p81

See strange – and grotesque – specimens p87

Head to an underground burial site p98

Climb a tower of fear p110

Hunt some ghosts p150

Call on the spirits p165

Jive to jazz in a torture chamber p176

Watch – and get involved – in a horror show p171

Party with the seven deadly sins p189

Set your sights on the Lock of the Dead p197

See hanging corpses p198

24:00

Midnight Movies

Get your fill of film at the midnight hour at **Le Champo Cinéma**, where you can watch not just one but three movies – and have breakfast, too! Choose from two concurrent programmes at this art-house cinema, founded in 1938 in an old bookstore. Then slide into the crimson-red chairs and away to fantasy until morning.

Le Champo Cinéma: 51 Rue des Écoles, 75005, +33 1 43 54 51 60. Métro: Odéon, Saint-Michel. Midnight movies every Saturday at 12 am. Price: €15 (€12 if purchased in advance); €6 concession. www.lechampo.com ⧗🎬

Go Ghetto

Nobody parties like the Brazilians, so if it's a truly wild time you're after you need to be at **Favela Chic** (*favela* means *ghetto* in Portuguese). Billed as a circus rather than a club or a bar, you can lose your head in the colourful clashing interior; dance to the resident DJs spinning mixtures of reggae, funk and soul; and chow down on traditional dishes from Brazil.

It's busy, it's buzzing and the music throbs – but if you're looking for a joyous night out that rivals the tropics, this just might be it.

Favela Chic Paris: 18 Rue du Faubourg du Temple, 75011, +33 1 40 21 38 14. Métro: République. Open: Tues to Thurs 8 pm to 2 am; Fri and Sat 8 pm to 4 am. www.favelachic.com/paris

Among Friends

For a down-home feeling you surely won't find in expensive cocktail joints, make your way to **Au Rendez-Vous des Amis**. Chilled out and friendly, you can read a book from one of the shelves, munch a plate of mixed meats or just down some wine.

You'll feel like you're with friends, even if everyone's a perfect stranger.

Au Rendez-Vous des Amis: 23 Rue Gabrielle, 75018, +33 1 46 06 01 60. Métro: Abbesses. Open: daily 8:30 am to 2 am. Happy hour 8 pm to 10 pm. www.myspace.com/rendezvousdesamis

Midnight Musings

Want to get existential? A favourite of Sartre and Beauvoir, at **Café de Flore** you can sit yourself down in the same seats as the great thinkers. The Art Deco interior hasn't changed since World War II and while the fare isn't cheap or particularly remarkable, it's worth a venture in to soak up the past. If you can, get a seat on the terrace and ponder the meaning of life as the world goes by.

Café de Flore: 172 Boulevard Saint-Germain, 75006, +33 1 45 48 55 26. Métro: Saint-Germain-des-Prés. Open: daily 7 am to 2 am. www.cafe-de-flore.com

Night Walk

It may have been a long night but don't worry: the coloured glass beads you see as you head for home aren't a hallucination. Two cupolas, made of glistening beads threaded through aluminium, hang over a bench right by the entrance of métro station **Palais-Royal**, one of the first eight stations to be opened in 1900. Artist Jean-Michel Othoniel designed the *Kiosque des noctambules* (Kiosk of the Nightwalkers) in 2000 to celebrate the Métro's 100th birthday.

Take a load off and join the party one more time before calling it a night.

Métro: Palais Royal–Musée du Louvre: entrance on Place Colette, 75001. Station open from around 5:45 am to 1 am (2 am on Fri and Sat).

Rock Shock

Billed as the 'ultimate rock bar' where the 'boring and bored' are banned, **Cantada II** sets expectations high. With rock, indie and punk music bizarrely combined with absinthe and medieval food, it definitely lives up to its hype. The red walls, chains and pictures of the seven deadly sins only serve to add to the surreal atmosphere. If it's hardcore you're looking for, you'll certainly feel at home here.

Cantada II: 13 Rue Moret, 75011, +33 1 48 05 96 89. Métro: Couronnes, Ménilmontant, Parmentier. Open: Mon to Thurs 6 pm to 1:30 am; Fri, Sat 6 pm to 5 am. www.cantada.net

24 Hour Fact
Crossing Paris by Métro takes about 35 minutes.

Celeb Spot

It's not cheap and it's got the snob factor galore (you wouldn't expect anything less from a building whose design mantra was 'all things in excess'), but if you're looking to see a celeb or two then **Hôtel Costes** is your best bet. Head straight to the bar just off the main lobby, where you might run into Kylie, Lindsay Lohan or the Beckhams. And even if you happen to hit a star-free night, the over-the-top gold-and-purple décor is enough to impress on its own. A note of caution though, Sunday best is recommended.

Hôtel Costes: 239 Rue Saint Honoré, 75001, +33 1 42 44 50 25. Métro: Concorde. Open: daily 7 pm to 2 am. Reservations recommended. www.hotelcostes.com

Oyster Aphrodisiac

If you need something extra to get going for the night ahead, you can't go wrong with oysters from **Au Rocher de Cancale**.

Located on the site of a former oyster market and open since 1846 – a time when Parisians were consuming six million dozen oysters each year – the restaurant was a favourite of literary giant Balzac and the street itself was immortalised in an 1878 painting by Claude Monet. Polish off some sea creatures and take a stroll through history.

Au Rocher de Cancale: 78 Rue Montorgueil, 75002, +33 1 42 33 50 29. Métro: Sentier, Étienne Marcel. Open: daily 8 am to 2 am. www.aurocherdecancale.fr 🦐

Very Curious

There's no beer at cocktail lounge **Curio Parlor** but there are plenty of other alcoholic concoctions to fill the gap. Sink down on the plush green sofas and sip your Strawberry Field under the blank-eyed stare of various taxidermy creatures. Or grab your Spiced Mule, nip into a nook and close the curtain for privacy.

With all there is to absorb here – from silent movies to butterflies – you might even forget that beer exists.

Curio Parlor: 16 Rue des Bernadins, 75005, +33 1 44 07 12 47. Métro: Maubert-Mutualité. Open: Mon to Thurs 7 pm to 2 am; Fri, Sat from 7 pm to 4 am. www.curioparlor.com

Porn-Art

Is it pornography or is it art? At the **Erotic Museum of Paris**, the line between the two is definitely blurred. Opened in 1997 and occupying seven floors of a townhouse in Montmartre, the museum showcases past and present erotic objects from around the world. Learn about the brothels of the nineteenth century, peer into doll-house peep-shows and see a porn film from the early 1900s. With exhibitions changing every three months, you can be sure your interest will stay, well, aroused.

Musée de l'Érotisme de Paris: 72 Boulevard de Clichy, 75018, +33 1 42 58 28 73. Métro: Blanche. Open: daily 10 am to 2 am. Price: €9. www.musee-erotisme.com

Best of Both Worlds

Fashioned after his two popular bars in New York, native Parisian Hervé Rousseau finally brought his champagne-bar concept home. **Flûte l'Étoile** combines New York glamour with the refined elegance of Paris – in other words, cocktails with champagne. Couples can cuddle in the curtained booths or groove out in the open to live jazz each Wednesday. Grab your drink from either side of the pond, sit back, and enjoy the pleasant mix of two very different cultures.

Flûte l'Étoile: 19 Rue de l'Étoile, 75017, +33 1 45 72 10 14. Métro: Charles de Gaulle-Étoile, Ternes. Open: Mon to Sat 5 pm to 2 am. www.flutebar.fr

Balls Up

Have energy to spare? At **Le Bowling Mouffetard**, you can throw some balls around in the eight bowling lanes until the early hours. Join in the theme nights, from Carnaval to Beaujolais, for extra fun. And if bowling's not your thing, you can always hit the billiards table.

Le Bowling Mouffetard: 73 Rue Mouffetard, 75005, +33 1 43 31 09 35. Métro: Place Monge. Open: Mon to Fri 3 pm to 2 am; Sat, Sun 10 am to 2 am. Price: from €3.30 to €6.50 per set; shoe hire €2. Under 16s must be accompanied by adults. www.bowlingmouffetard.fr

Who are you, Polly Maggoo?

Although its new mosaic-tiled exterior belies its past as a down-at-the-heels hang-out for rock stars (reputedly Jim Morrison was a regular) and 1968 student revolutionaries, **Polly Maggoo** still serves up a good helping of fun at all hours. Named after a 1960s French film mocking the fashion world, the bar itself has fallen prey to its yuppie surroundings. Even so, it's worth a visit for its late-night tapas, salsa and buzzing weekend atmosphere.

Polly Maggoo: 3-5 Rue du Petit Pont, 75005, +33 1 46 33 33 64. Métro: Cluny-La Sorbonne. Open: daily 10:30 am to 2 am. 🍸

02:00

Oui Madame!

If you still have cash and you're up for more, **Club MadaM** keeps the party going until morning. Open until 6 am on Fridays and Saturdays, you can dance to live music and DJs until you drop at this small but perfectly formed underground club. Be prepared to wait in line and be crushed on the dance floor once you're in, though. This is where the cool kids go to groove and there's a price to pay to join them.

Club MadaM: 128 Rue La Boétie, 75008, +33 1 53 76 02 11. Métro: Franklin D. Roosevelt or George V. Open: Thurs 7 pm to 2 am; Fri, Sat 11:30 pm to 6 am, Sun 10:30 pm to 4 am. www.madam.fr

Ant Hill

By day it buzzes with coffee drinkers, but at night the industrial-styled **La Fourmi** (The Ant) is a hive of activity as those still with energy swarm in for a few cheap beverages and a place to deconstruct the night. Climb up to the mezzanine where you can be the king of the hill or just perch on a stool at the ground floor's zinc bar. Grab a flyer from the pile to see what's on and plan your next move.

La Fourmi: 74 Rue des Martyrs, 75018, +33 1 42 64 70 35. Métro: Pigalle. Open: Mon to Thurs 8 am to 2 am; Fri, Sat 8 am to 4 am; Sun 10 am to 2 am.

Metal Head

Rock n' roll's not dead yet, and if you're looking for proof just head over to **Les Furieux**, where on Fridays and Saturdays you can fill your ears until 5 am. Come for the happy hour from 6 pm to 8 pm, scan the photographic exhibition lining the walls, and swallow some absinthe. Then let the sounds of post-punk, gothic, industrial and metal fill your ears.

Les Furieux: 74 Rue de la Roquette, 75011, +33 1 47 00 78 44. Métro: Bastille or Voltaire. Open: Tues to Thurs 4 pm to 2 am; Fri, Sat 4 pm to 5 am; Sun 7 pm to 2 am. www.lesfurieux.fr

Be Selective

It's full of tourists now, but from the early to mid-twentieth century **Le Select** was the place for artists to eat, sleep (waiters were told not to wake them) and argue. Opened in 1925, the café was a favourite of Henry Miller, who wrote about it in *The Tropic of Cancer*. Hemingway and Picasso were regulars, too. It was the first café in Montparnasse to stay open all night, and even today you can still visit in the wee hours.

Le Select: 99 Boulevard du Montparnasse, 75006, +33 1 45 48 38 24. Métro: Vavin. Open: Sun to Thurs 7 am to 2 am; Fri, Sat 7 am to 4 am. 🍸

Dance on Deck

For more than ten years, big red boat **Batofar** has been home to some of Paris' best after-hours parties. With DJs spinning everything from experimental to techno, you can join the crowd on the dance-floor or hang around in one of the suspended hammocks on deck. Just watch where you spin or you might end up in the drink!

Batofar: 11 Quai François-Mauriac, 75013, +33 1 53 60 17 30. Métro: Bibliothèque François Mitterrand, Quai de la Gare. Club open Wed to Sat 11 pm to 6 am; terrace Tues to Sat 9 pm onwards. Price: free entry for terrace before 11 pm; from €10 for the club. www.batofar.org

Do the Cha Cha

Keep your feet moving at the **Chacha Club**, where you can get a cocktail, take a spin on the dance floor and have a bath in the giant loo complete with tub. Run by the same team behind the ultra-cool café Hôtel du Nord, even if you aren't crazy about dancing you can tuck yourself away in one of the many nooks, drink in the thirties-inspired décor, and let the music do the talking.

Chacha Club: 47 Rue Berger, 75001, +33 1 40 13 12 12. Métro: Louvre-Rivoli. Open: Mon to Sat 8 pm to 6 am; restaurant open 8 pm to 12 am. www.chachaclub.fr

Dead Lock

If it's dark and it's late then it's the perfect time to check out the **Lock of the Dead** on Canal Saint-Martin. Located near a Merovingian cemetery and the infamous Montfaucon gallows – where offenders were hanged in groups of sixteen and left to rot – if you close your eyes you may still catch a whiff of the scent of decay. In this café-packed area, though, it's more likely to be last night's dinner than what's leftover on the gallows.

Les Écluses des Morts: Rue Louis Blanc on Canal Saint-Martin, 75010. Métro: Louis Blanc.

Over 18

Open from midnight onwards, dance the night into morning at **Le Club 18**. The oldest gay bar in Paris – with room for only a hundred souls – it may get kind of cosy but nothing beats its good-time vibe. Get your free drink in hand, groove to the mixture of dance, electronic and pop, and be pleasantly squashed.

Le Club 18: 18 Rue de Beaujolais, 75001 +33 1 42 97 52 13. Métro: Palais Royal–Musée du Louvre, Pyramides. Open: Fri, Sat 12 am to 6 am. Price: €10 (includes one drink). www.club18.fr

Rat Catchers

The store's only open by day, but if you're hankering after a little late-night taxidermy, fill your eyes at **Julien Aurouze and Co**. The exterminator's shop-front clearly displays their expertise: dead rats dangle in the window and the sign above promises to destroy 'harmful animals'. Open since 1872, the shop also featured in the Disney film *Ratatouille.*

Julien Aurouze and Co: 8 Rue des Halles, 75001, +33 1 40 41 16 20. Métro: Châtelet. Open: Mon to Sat 9 am to 12:30 pm; 2 pm to 6:30 pm. www.aurouze.fr

All Loved Up

If you fancy some late night loving, head to the **French Love** bar. Although it's no longer a place where women relieve men of their cash in exchange for kisses, it's still under the same ownership and vestiges of its former self remain. Ring the buzzer and let the chandeliers, gold tiles and some rather absorbing paintings seduce you. If you want to stay out of sight, get cosy in the telephone box *cum fumoir*. Either way, be prepared to pay for the privilege. You can't shell out anymore for some actual loving, but the drinking ain't cheap.

French Love: 37 Rue de Ponthieu, 75008. Métro: Saint-Philippe-du-Roule. Open: daily 8 pm to 6 am.

Fakers

It may be late but your eyes do not deceive you: the two rows of windows painted on a nondescript building on the corner of **Rue Quincampoix** and **Aubry le Boucher** aren't real, despite their initial appearance.

Run your gaze over the detailed artistry and marvel at the optical illusion.

Phantom Windows: corner of Rue Quincampoix and Aubry le Boucher, 75004. Métro: Châtelet or Rambuteau.

For Whom the Bell Tolls

If it's your stomach that's making alarming noises, head to **La Cloche D'Or** (The Golden Bell) to tide you over 'til morning. Once a hang-out for Edith Piaf, Cocteau and Kessel, it remains a draw for nearby Moulin Rouge dancers and actors, with Depeche Mode spotted, too. Grab a seat on one of the three floors, warm your hands by the fire and feast on the filling fare from foie gras to steak tartar.

La Cloche D'Or: 3 Rue Mansart, 75009, +33 1 48 74 48 88. Métro: Blanche or Pigalle. Open: Mon to Sat until 4 am. www.alaclochedor.com

24 Hour Fact
Walking from Notre Dame to the Louvre takes 15 minutes.

04:00

Maybe It's Mabillon

There's nothing too remarkable about this cocktail bar and restaurant, but if you're looking for a late-night drink and a great terrace to sit and sip near Saint-Germain, then **Mabillon** is the place to go. Open every day until dawn, you can relax under the patio heaters and watch the night-time fade into morning.

Café Mabillon: 164 Boulevard Saint-Germain, 75006, +33 1 43 26 62 93. Métro: Mabillon, Saint-Germain-des-Prés, Odéon. Open: daily 7:30 am to 5:30 am. 🍸

Champ Champers

See the Eiffel Tower sparkle and sip some bubbly at **Parc Champ de Mars**. One of the largest parks in Paris, it was originally used by the École Militaire for military drills. Today, it features winding paths, ponds and lots of benches to gaze upon its greatest feature: the Eiffel Tower. With no gates – and therefore no closing time – it's a great place to see the

Tower light up, no matter the hour. Listen for the cry of the tawny owl at night; this park is one of the few places where the elusive bird can be found.

Parc Champ de Mars: access from Quai Branly and Avenue de la Motte-Picquet, 75007. Métro: École Militaire. Open: daily 24 hours.

The Main Drag

Held twice a month at concert hall **Bataclan**, these crazy no-holds-barred parties feature drag queens galore, dancing and a whole lot of fun. *La Nuit des Follivores* (with French music from the 70s and 80s) and its sister *La Nuit des Crazyvores* (with English music from the 70s, 80s and 90s) have been going strong for ten years and continue to be packed with every kind of humanity. Get your gear on for this gay-friendly event and join in the revelry.

La Nuit des Follivores and La Nuit des Crazyvores: Bataclan, 50 Boulevard Voltaire, 75011, +33 1 43 14 00 30. Métro: Oberkampf. Held twice a month from 11:45 pm to dawn. Price: €18 (includes one drink). www.follivores.com; www.le-bataclan.com

Last Supper

It's not the best bistro fare you'll find, but if you're in need of some soup or steak to absorb last night's damage – or you want some carbs to kick off the day – you can get it at **Le Tambour**. Open through the night until 6 am, fulfil your chitterlings cravings or chow-down on pigs-feet amidst the eccentric décor of fire hydrants and random street signs.

Le Tambour: 41 Rue Montmartre, 75002, +33 1 42 33 06 90. Métro: Sentier. Open: Tues to Sat 12 pm to 6 am; Sun, Mon 6 pm to 6 am. 🐷

Pig Out

You needn't worry about looking like a porker at this restaurant: at **Au Pied de Cochon**, it's all about the pig. Open 24 hours since 1946, you can chow down on the legendary onion soup by day or sample a swine delight by night. Located just beside Les Halles, it's the ideal place to refuel after late-night cinema or gear-up with extra calories for clubbing. Grab some trotters or some bone marrow; if pigs could fly, you can bet they'd stop here for some sustenance too.

Au Pied de Cochon: 6 Rue Coquillière, 75001, +33 1 40 13 77 00. Métro: Les Halles. Open: daily, 24 hours. www.pieddecochon.com 🐷

Get Shorty

Squeeze in one last bit of fun even if your stamina's flagging by sauntering down Paris' shortest street, the **Rue Des Degrés** in the second *arrondissement*. At only 5.75 metres long and consisting of 14 steps, you'll reach the end before you know it.

Rue des Degrés: connecting Rue de Cléry and Rue Beauregard, 75002. Métro: Bonne Nouvelle.

It's That Time

Tempus fugit when you're having fun, but stop for a second to take in Paris' oldest public clock on the **Tour de l'Horloge** at the Conciergerie, on the corner of the Quai de l'Horloge and the Pont au Change. Although it may be hard to tell the time in the dark, the clock's ornate fleur-de-lis frame is worth a look. First constructed in 1370, the clock before you dates from 1535. Put the night on pause and ponder bygone times.

Paris' First Public Clock: Tour de l'Horloge, corner of Quai de l'Horloge and Pont au Change, 75001. Métro: Cité.

Board the Bus

Missed the last métro? Spent your cash on clubbing? Hop aboard night-bus service **Noctilien** to get back to your bed. With over 40 routes, the service runs through many Paris hotspots and suburbs, connecting to most major transport hubs. From around 12:30 am to 5:30 am (depending on the route), a single ticket costs €1.60. Watch the city lights flash by as you head for home.

Noctilien: www.noctilien.fr. Service runs from around 12:30 am to 5:30 am. Price: single ticket €1.60.

House of Gold

If the night has almost bankrupted you but you're in the mood for more luxury, clap your eyes on the **Golden House.** Once Paris' most extravagant restaurant, the building's name comes from its gold-plated façade. The nineteenth-century restaurant, with over 80,000 bottles of wine in its cellar and private compartments for the super-rich, was frequented by the future King Edward VII along with other members of the French upper-class.

Although the restaurant closed in 1902 it's still a golden house in more than just name: today, it's the corporate headquarters for bank BNP Paribas. Rub your eyes and dream of your pot of gold.

Maison Dorée: 20 Boulevard des Italiens, 75009. Métro: Richelieu–Drouot.

Hit the Wall

Blink and you might miss it: a leg, a torso and a man's head coming out of a wall. Tucked away in the winding streets of Montmartre, this sculpture – **Le Passe-Muraille** (or Walker through Walls, in English) – depicts one of writer Marcel Aymé's most well-known characters, a man who uses his newfound talent for less than altruistic means.

A nearby resident until his death in 1967, Aymé was interested in the dark side of the human character. Pause for a second and ponder what you'd do with superpowers.

Le Passe-Muraille: Place Marcel-Aymé (corner of Allée des Brouillards and Rue Norvins), 75018. Métro: Lamarck – Caulaincourt or Abbesses.

24 Hour Fact

A trip on the Montmartre funicular, which covers a vertical distance of 36 metres and a track of 108 metres, takes less than 90 seconds.

24 Hours of Luxury

Stroll by a country chateau p23

Get your own green tour p117

Check out some crystal couture p39

Purchase eye candy p41

Conjure up your own fabric creation p52

Stuff yourself at a pig paradise p54

Fork out for serious dough p70

Get glam with Guerlin p62

Kit out your posh pooch p89

Gulp water with Swarovski p86

Fashion some head gear p116

Buzz over the city in style p127

Sip your drink in an indoor garden p179

Lounge around in one-armed chairs p180

Dance the cha-cha p197

Lay your eyes on a house of gold 205

INDEX

24 Hours London MARSHA MOORE £9.99

ISBN: 978-0-956-122-9-2

The first in the series, the 2010/2011 Edition of 24 Hours London gives you
the quirky, cool and downright crazy stuff that London has to offer, no matter
what time of the day or night.

The Reluctant Traveller   BILL LUMLEY £9.99

ISBN: 978-0-956-122-5-4

He enraged the nation in Home Truths, now Lumley is heading for Ethiopia,
where he is desperately trying to avoid all strenuous activity as he is forced
to help find and climb a treacherous lost mountain.

Naked in Knightsbridge NICKY SCHMIDT £7.99

ISBN: 978-0-956-122- , 3

Jools Grand is not known for going the extra mile, so when she loses her
cleaning business after a rather nasty fire, she decides the easiest way to get
back on top is by auctioning herself in marriage online. Unfortunately for
Jools, things don't exactly go to plan.

The Dresskeeper MARY NAYLUS £6.99   ISBN: 978-0-956-122-8-5

13-year-old Picky Robson hates her life, so when she puts on a vintage dress
in Gran's attic and finds herself back in 1685, she welcomes the adventure, in
spite of the wig-wearing maniac who is stalking her.

The Littlest Detective in London SUZY BROWNLEE £5.99

ISBN: 978-0-956-122-0-9

Follow Clementine Cordelia Bird and her nemesis Natasha Commonov as
they struggle to find their missing parents in this black comedy for girls aged
9-12 years. First in a series of eight.